COTEHELE

Cornwall

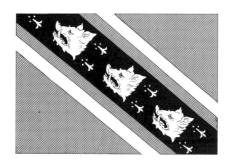

THE NATIONAL TRUST

This new book draws on the first Cotehele guidebook written by James Lees-Milne and on subsequent editions by Michael Trinick. John Cornforth kindly made available an advance draft of his recent articles on the furnishing of Cotehele. Chapter Two and the architectural sections of Chapters Three and Four have been written by KEYSTONE, Historic Building Consultants of Exeter; Chapter Five by Wendy Hefford of the Department of Textile Furnishings and Dress at the Victoria & Albert Museum; Chapter Six by Karin Walton of the Bristol City Art Gallery; Chapter Seven by F. Wilkinson, formerly of the Tower Armouries; Chapter Eleven by John Stengelhofen, formerly of the National Maritime Museum; all the other sections have been written or revised by National Trust staff. The Trust also gratefully acknowledges the support of English Heritage, which has grant-aided restoration of the tapestries, and of Maureen Attrill and the staff of the Plymouth City Museum and Art Gallery. The extract from Queen Charlotte's diary is quoted by gracious permission of Her Majesty the Queen.

Conservation: The house can be extremely dark inside. There has never been electric light in the old rooms and the Trust feels that this contributes to their atmosphere. The lack of light also accounts for the fact that many of the textiles still retain remarkably fresh and vivid colours. On dark days the Trust tries to be flexible in its use of the sun curtains, but asks visitors to accept the house in its natural state and not to expect to view objects in museum conditions. To protect the fragile contents of Cotehele, the Trust regrets that large hand- and other bags are not allowed inside the house; they should be left with the stewards at the front door.

First published in Great Britain in 1991 by the National Trust

Chapters 1–4, 6–12 © 1991 The National Trust: Chapter 5 © 1991 Wendy Hefford
Reprinted 1997

ISBN 0 07078 0117 6

Photographs: City of Bristol Museum and Art Gallery page 22; *Country Life* pages
7, 24, 60, 62, 67, 68; National Gallery of Art, Washington/James Pipkin page 15; NT pages
13, 17, 23, 27, 31, 34, 35, 41, 55, 57 (bottom), 64, 65, 66 (top), 69, 72, 76, 77, 80, 83, 87,
88, 89, 92, 93; NT/Robert Chapman pages 9, 30 (top), 54, 61, 66 (bottom), 85; NT/John
Hammond page 74; NT/Angelo Hornak pages 37, 39, 40, 42, 43 (top and bottom),
45, 46, 47, 48, 50 (top and bottom), 51, 52; NT/George Wright pages 12, 14,
16, 19 (bottom), 57 (top), 91; NT/Jeremy Whitaker page 75; Plymouth City Museum and Art
Gallery, Mount Edgcumbe House Collection front cover, pages 4, 18, 19 (top), 20, 21, 25, 26, 28,
29, 30 (bottom), 32, 73, 79, 81, 86, 94, back cover; Woodmansterne page 49.

Designed by James Shurmer

Phototypeset by BAS Printers Limited, Over Wallop, Hampshire

Colour reproduction by Acculith 76, Barnet, Hertfordshire

Printed in Italy by Amilcare Pizzi s.p.a. for
the National Trust, 36 Queen Anne's Gate, London SW1H 9AS
Registered charity no. 205846

CONTENTS

INTRODUCTION

The ancient manor house of Cotehele, its Great Hall hung with armour and its cold and dimly lit rooms rich with tapestry, exudes a strong air of romantic antiquity. The life of the man who built it, Sir Richard Edgcumbe, is the stuff of legend – the very ideal of the concept of English chivalry in the late Middle Ages. Much of the surrounding estate is still cultivated in the traditional manner for which the Tamar valley has been noted for centuries – bulb growing, market gardening and smallhold farming. The river is still netted for salmon on the wide bend below the quay; the woods continue to be managed for commercial crops as well as for public access, and the presence at the quay of an old Tamar barge provides an active link with the time when the river was the main artery of the estate and the quay was alive with the bustle of shipping; the forge in the Blacksmith's Shop still glows as a reminder of days when the making of cartwheels and horseshoes was essential to the running of the estate; the lime kilns bear witness to the days when lump lime was brought up the river from Plymouth to enrich the land; the old inn, the Edgcumbe Arms, continues to provide refreshment for visitors.

The estuary of the River Tamar is still best explored by boat and then on foot. While narrow lanes plunge down to the several quays which once served the private estates and small rural communities on both banks, there is no road running up either side of the valley. This remoteness has also inhibited modern housing developments along the estuary, and a journey up or down the lower river still presents today an unspoilt picture little changed from its appearance centuries ago.

Until the opening of the Tamar Bridge at Saltash in 1961, the first road to cross the river was that running west from Tavistock to Callington (the present A390) over the dramatically sited, early sixteenth-century New Bridge at Gunnislake. From New Bridge the road rises steeply to the top of the hill, where the old way to Cotehele forked left and thence down through the lanes to the ancient farm of Trehill. Here there was a gate into the medieval deer park. The track, now grassed over, still runs through the fields and leads to the west side of the Edgcumbe family's ancient home.

'The Court Dinner at Cotehele', by Nicholas Condy c.1840 (Plymouth City Museum and Art Gallery, Mount Edgcumbe House Collection)

CHAPTER ONE
THE FIRST EDGCUMBES
AT COTEHELE

Cotehele gave its name to the family who owned the estate from the latter part of the thirteenth century, and parts of the house built by the de Coteheles probably survive under later remodelling. On the death of William de Cotehele, before 1336, his two children, Ralph and Hilaria, were made wards of the lord of the manor of Calstock, John, Earl of Cornwall, brother to King Edward III. Ralph died a minor and Hilaria thus became the owner of Cotehele. In 1353 she married William Edgcumbe, declaring by petition that she would have none other. Thus Cotehele passed into the hands of the Edgcumbe family, who were to remain its owners for the next six centuries.

The Edgcumbes were of ancient Devon origin, their name deriving from Eggescombe or Edgecombe (now called Nether Edgcumbe) in the parish of Milton Abbot to the north of Tavistock. An ancient manor house still stands there, with a stone over the gateway engraved with the arms of the family, the date 1292 and the initials 'RE' for Richard Edgcumbe. Within a year of the death of William Edgcumbe in 1379–80, Hilaria married William Fleete of Sutton, in Plymouth. They lived at Cotehele for the rest of their lives, after which it reverted to her son by her first marriage, Peter Edgcumbe. Her Christian name lives on in the Edgcumbe family, at present in the person of Lady Hilaria Gibbs, a daughter of the 6th Earl of Mount Edgcumbe.

Peter Edgcumbe seems to have died without issue, for he was succeeded by a William Edgcumbe, who appears to have been his younger brother. William represented Plymouth in the Parliament of 1446–7. For the next four centuries an Edgcumbe held a West Country seat in almost every parliament for which records survive and the family played a central role in the politics of the region. William, in his turn, was succeeded by another

Peter Edgcumbe who married Elizabeth, daughter and heiress of Richard Holland. It was their eldest son, Richard, who was the first member of the family to achieve more than local renown.

In Cornish history Richard Edgcumbe (d.1489) has become a heroic and almost legendary figure. We first hear of him involved in a bitter feud with a neighbour, Richard Willoughby of Bere Ferrers, whose estates across the River Tamar were, oddly enough, to pass to the Edgcumbes in the late eighteenth century through the marriage of the 2nd Earl of Mount Edgcumbe to Lady Sophia Hobart, daughter of the 2nd Earl of Buckinghamshire, of Blickling Hall in Norfolk. We read that as Richard Edgcumbe was quietly riding home from a friend's house to Cotehele, Willoughby, with 34 armed men, lay in ambush to murder him – 'contrewayted the said Richard to have murdered him'. On another occasion Willoughby's armed ruffians assaulted Cotehele House, which they tried to burn, and beat one of Edgecumbe's servants 'to the hurt and damage of . . . twenty pounds and more'. In spite of these unpromising beginnings the two men subsequently became the best of friends.

In 1483 Richard Edgcumbe, perhaps prompted by rumours that Richard III had murdered the two sons of Edward IV in the Tower of London, took the boldest step of his life by declaring himself in league against the Crown. Exeter was the rallying point for the disaffected forces under Henry Stafford, Duke of Buckingham, who was at once defeated and executed without trial. Edgcumbe, who had by then sufficiently compromised himself, was outlawed but lay in hiding at Cotehele. Here he was pursued by the King's local agent, Sir Henry Trenowth of Bodrugan, who for years past had been the terror of these parts of Cornwall. So feared and hated was he that a number of the Cornish gentry had already petitioned the King to relieve

Painting of the tomb of Sir Richard Edgcumbe at Morlaix in Brittany, which was destroyed in the French Revolution (Chapel)

the neighbourhood of his cruelty and depredations. Trenowth soon tracked Edgcumbe to his retreat, and while he drew a cordon round the house, posted a watch at the gatehouse. Edgcumbe managed to slip through the net cast for him, and having cut the throat of a luckless sentry, fled down what is now the garden towards the river's edge, hotly pursued by Trenowth. But Edgcumbe was as wily as he was active. With his pursuers almost upon him, he tore off his cap, put a stone into it and dropped it into the water. And so, in the words of the early seventeenth-century historian of Cornwall, Richard Carew, the pursuers, 'looking down after the noise, and seeing his cap swimming thereon,

supposed that he had desperately drowned himself, and gave over their further hunting'. Meanwhile the fugitive remained hidden in the undergrowth and eventually slipped away by sea to Brittany. A few years later Edgcumbe returned and in grateful memory of this incident built upon the spot a chapel in honour of SS. George and Thomas à Becket, which still stands. It was restored in 1620 and again in 1769. It preserves a fine original doorway, resembling those which Edgcumbe built at the house, and a number of late Gothic pew ends.

In Brittany, Richard Edgcumbe joined forces with Henry Tudor and became one of his closest supporters and friends. He fought for him at the Battle of Bosworth in 1485, and, as a reward for his loyalty, was knighted and made Controller of the Royal Household when Henry became king. Nemesis finally overcame Trenowth. His estates

were confiscated and given by Henry VII to Edgcumbe, who had the added satisfaction of turning
the tables on his old enemy, by chasing him into
the sea. The beautiful headland between Mevagis-
sey and The Dodman, now known as Bodrugan's
Leap (and also owned by the National Trust), com-
memorates the spot where Bodrugan met his death.

For the remaining four years of his life, Edgcumbe lived in great prosperity. His continued
services under the Crown included an embassy in
Calais to accept the allegiance of its burghers and
the generalship of the royalist troops in the Battle
of Stoke in 1487. In 1488 he was made Ambassador
to Scotland and soon afterwards was sent to Ireland
to accept the allegiance of the chieftains, his account
of which is still to be seen at the University Library
at Clogher, Co. Louth.

During the brief intervals he spent at Cotehele,
Edgcumbe extended the medieval house his family
had inherited from the de Coteheles (see Chapter
Two). In 1489 he set out upon his last journey, having made his will and consigned his soul to St
Thomas à Becket. He died that year at Morlaix, in
Brittany, whither he had gone to fight for Anne
of Brittany in the company of his old neighbour
from Bere Ferrers, lately created Lord Willoughby
de Broke. Edgcumbe was buried at Morlaix but all
trace of his tomb has vanished.

Sir Richard Edgcumbe was succeeded in his
estates by his son, Piers (1468/9–1539), who was
awarded the Order of the Bath at the marriage of
Prince Arthur with Katherine of Aragon and was
later present at the victories of Tournay, Terouanne
and the Battle of Spurs. For his bravery in battle
he was created knight-banneret by Henry VIII in
1513. Sir Piers was one of the leading landowners
in the South West, and his first marriage, in 1493,
to Joan Durnford, heiress to lands on both sides of
the Tamar near Plymouth, increased his influence
in the area. He tried to expand his estate still further
at the Dissolution of the Monasteries in the 1530s
by laying claim to Totnes Priory and Cornworthy
Nunnery, which had been founded by his ancestors,
but without success. The combined wealth of Sir
Piers and his wife enabled him to complete his
father's building operations, which lasted until his
own death in 1539. His finest achievement at Cote-

hele is the Great Hall, in one of the windows of
which appear the Edgcumbe arms impaling those
of Durnford, thus suggesting that the room was
finished before her death in 1520.

Among the properties which Joan Durnford
brought to the Edgcumbe family was the Mount
Edgcumbe estate at the mouth of the Tamar. Sir
Piers enclosed the park at Mount Edgcumbe and
in 1553, his son, Richard, built a new house on the
estate, which from then on became the family's
principal seat. It was this decision that helped to
ensure that the main structure of the house built at
Cotehele by Sir Richard and Sir Piers would survive
with so little alteration.

*(Right) The Chapel in the Wood, built by Sir Richard
Edgcumbe in the 1480s to give thanks for his escape from
Sir Henry Trenowth*

THE EDGCUMBES OF COTEHELE

Hilaria de Cotehele = (1) William Edgcumbe (d.1379/80)
m.1353
= (2) William Fleete

Peter Edgcumbe   William Edgcumbe (d.1434) MP

Peter Edgcumbe = Elizabeth, dau. of Richard Holland

Sir Richard Edgcumbe = Joan (d.1500), dau. of Thomas Tremayne
(d.1489) Knight-banneret, MP   of Collacombe

Elizabeth, grandmother of Sir Walter Ralegh

Sir Piers Edgcumbe = (1) Joan (d.1520), dau. of James Durnford of East Stonehouse, Devon
(1468/9–1539)   m.1493
Knight-banneret, MP   = (2) Catherine (d.1553), dau. of Sir John St John of Bletsoe,
                              widow of Sir Griffith ap Rhys m.1530

Sir Richard Edgcumbe = (1) Elizabeth, dau. of Sir John Arundell
(c.1499–1562) MP   m.1516
                         = (2) Elizabeth, dau. of John Tregian
                         = (3) Winifred, dau. of Sir William Essex

Sir Piers Edgcumbe = Margaret, dau. of Sir Andrew Luttrell of Dunster, Somerset
(by 1536–1607/8) MP   m.c.1555

Margaret (1560–1648)★† = Sir Edward Denny

Sir Richard Edgcumbe = (1) Anne Cary (d.1607)
(c.1570–1638) MP   m.1602
                         = (2) Mary (d.1620), dau. of Sir Thomas Coteel★
                              m.1608

Col. Piers Edgcumbe = Mary,★ dau. of Sir John Glanville
(c.1610–67) MP   m.1636

Sir Richard Edgcumbe = Lady Anne Montagu (d.1729), dau. of Edward, 1st Earl of Sandwich
(1640–88) MP★   m.1671

Richard Edgcumbe = Matilda Furnese (1699–1721)
(1680–1758) MP   m.1715
cr. 1st Baron Edgcumbe 1742

Piers
(1676–94)

Piers

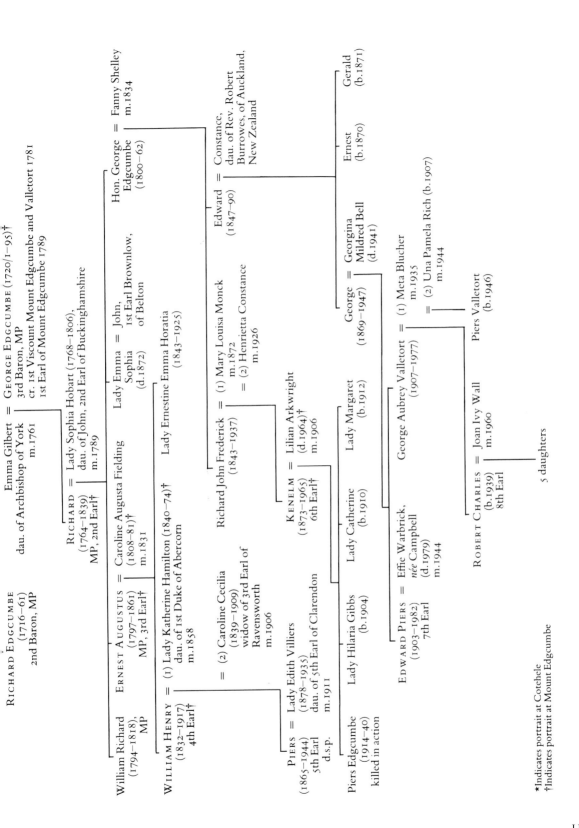

RICHARD EDGCUMBE (1716–61) 2nd Baron, MP = EMMA GILBERT dau. of Archbishop of York m.1761

GEORGE EDGCUMBE (1720/1–95)† 3rd Baron, MP cr. 1st Viscount Mount Edgcumbe and Valletort 1781 1st Earl of Mount Edgcumbe 1789

RICHARD (1764–1839), MP, 2nd Earl† = Lady Sophia Hobart (1768–1806), dau. of John, 2nd Earl of Buckinghamshire m.1789

Lady Emma Sophia (d.1872) = John, 1st Earl Brownlow, of Belton

Hon. George Edgcumbe (1800–62) = Fanny Shelley m.1834

Edward (1847–90) = Constance, dau. of Rev. Robert Burrowes, of Auckland, New Zealand

ERNEST AUGUSTUS (1797–1861) MP, 3rd Earl† = Caroline Augusta Fielding (1808–81)† m.1831

WILLIAM HENRY (1832–1917) 4th Earl† = (1) Lady Katherine Hamilton (1840–74)† dau. of 1st Duke of Abercorn m.1858
= (2) Caroline Cecilia (1839–1909) widow of 3rd Earl of Ravensworth m.1906

Lady Ernestine Emma Horatia (1843–1925)

Richard John Frederick (1843–1937) = (1) Mary Louisa Monck m.1872
= (2) Henrietta Constance m.1926

George (1869–1947) = Georgina Mildred Bell (d.1941)

Ernest (b.1870)

Gerald (b.1871)

William Richard (1794–1818), MP

PIERS (1865–1944) 5th Earl d.s.p. = Lady Edith Villiers (1878–1935) dau. of 5th Earl of Clarendon m.1911

KENELM (1873–1965) 6th Earl† = Lilian Arkwright (d.1964)† m.1906

Lady Margaret (b.1912)

George Aubrey Valletort (1907–1977) = (1) Meta Blucher m.1935
= (2) Una Pamela Rich (b.1907) m.1944

Piers Edgcumbe (1914–40) killed in action

Lady Hilaria Gibbs (b.1904)

EDWARD PIERS (1903–1982) 7th Earl = Effie Warbrick, née Campbell (d.1979) m.1944

Lady Catherine (b.1910)

Piers Valletort (b.1946)

ROBERT CHARLES (b.1939) 8th Earl = Joan Ivy Wall m.1960

5 daughters

*Indicates portrait at Cotehele
†Indicates portrait at Mount Edgcumbe

11

CHAPTER TWO
THE BUILDING OF COTEHELE

Hidden among the woods above the Calstock reach of the River Tamar, Cotehele seems remote from the modern world. Architecturally, time also appears to have stood still, thanks largely to the remarkably unaltered state of the house and the durability of the local granite and slatestone out of which it is built. Although other important manor houses in Cornwall – Roscarrock in St Endellion parish, Tonacombe in Morwenstow and the unfinished and abandoned complex at Trecarrel in Lezant parish – share some of its qualities, Cotehele is unique in showing few obvious signs of rebuilding since the mid-seventeenth century. Its com-

pleteness is the result of historical accident; the decision by the Edgcumbes to build a new family seat, Mount Edgcumbe, in 1553. This relieved Cotehele of most of the pressures of changing fashion and standards of comfort that alter and shape any house in full use over the centuries. In spite of the move to Mount Edgcumbe, Cotehele was not allowed to fall into dereliction, nor was it sold out of the family and reduced by partial demolition to farmhouse size, the fate of some ancient manor houses in the South West.

The local materials out of which Cotehele is constructed create its strongly regional character. The

The north-west corner of the Hall Court. The west range (left) may be the remains of the medieval building adapted by Sir Richard and Sir Piers Edgcumbe. At the angle the lancet window of the new Chapel meets the north range containing the Great Parlour crosswing and the Hall

The south front of Cotehele

house is built of brown and grey slatestone rubble, ubiquitous in Cornwall, with some granite ashlar masonry and dressings. Neither material takes a fine finish. Slatestone is only quarried in small blocks and, whether used in local churches or farmhouses, has an inevitably homespun quality. The sheer intractable hardness of granite gives a rustic quality to any carved detail, and even at its finest, on the church of St Mary Magdalene at Launceston, the effect is robust rather than delicate.

The present house incorporates parts of the fabric of the medieval house of the de Cotehele family which was transformed in the late fifteenth and sixteenth centuries by the Edgcumbes – principally Sir Richard and his son, Sir Piers – into a complex triple court-plan house. The appearance of the pre-Tudor

house and the precise extent to which its old walls and plan were retained by Sir Richard and Sir Piers remain a matter of debate, as no building accounts survive before the mid-seventeenth century. It has been suggested that the west range is the medieval core of the building. Certainly the rubble masonry differs from much of the stonework elsewhere, but there are no dateable details earlier than the late fifteenth century and the narrow one-light windows to the main court are not necessarily evidence of an early date. When examined closely the variation and patching in the masonry is a reminder of just how much minor piecemeal alteration and maintenance work has been carried out on the fabric over the centuries.

Sir Richard Edgcumbe is certainly unlikely to have undertaken a programme of mass demolition and building afresh – this would have been neither convenient nor thrifty. Old walling and parts of the earlier building that could be remodelled to new standards of convenience and status would have been retained. The siting of the old Cotehele mansion also played an important part in determining the plan of the new Edgcumbe house.

The arrangement is inward-looking, the main ranges opening on to enclosed courts with only small windows in the outer walls, suggesting a semi-defensive function. This characteristic may originate from pre-Tudor times, but may equally have been a response to the unstable politics of Cornwall in the late fifteenth and sixteenth centuries. Contemporary documents chart the lawlessness of great

landowners in the county in the late fifteenth century and there were Cornish rebellions in 1497, 1548 and 1549. Fluctuations in the tin trade throughout the period also posed threats to security, and as late as 1568 the West Country tin miners were described as a 'rough and mutinous multitude'. The Edgcumbes held Crown appointments. Sir Piers, for instance, was one of the members of the Council in the West, which was created in 1539 to bring the West Country more firmly under royal control. They were wise, therefore, to establish a secure house at Cotehele.

The Chapel is likely to have been the first project in the major rebuilding of Cotehele by Sir Richard

The Chapel with its bellcote, rebuilt by the Edgcumbes

and Sir Piers Edgcumbe. A chapel at Cotehele was licensed as early as 1411 and there may have been one before that date. If it stood on the same site, it was massively rebuilt in the late fifteenth century, the date of the Perpendicular Gothic traceried window to the main court. The barrel-vaulted type of roof construction in the Chapel is found in countless other late medieval church roofs in Devon and Cornwall. The ornate granite bellcote over the west end, however, has few parallels. It is similar to the bellcote of the chapel of St Mary at South Zeal on the northern fringe of Dartmoor, and the holy well at Dupath, near Callington, is crowned with a similar but simplified version.

After the Chapel the next phase in the programme of rebuilding Cotehele was the adjoining north range, which dates from the early sixteenth century, although it may represent a re-casting of an earlier building on the same site. The abrupt juxtaposition of the walls in the north-west corner marks an obvious transition between the building of the Chapel and the north range, which contains the Hall, rising through two storeys, to the east and, alongside at the higher end, a crosswing containing the Great Parlour with the principal Chamber above. The granite ashlar used on the exterior marks out the superior status of these rooms, and the Hall doorframe, positioned in line with the gatehouse entrance, is designed to impress the visitor with its distinctive carved granite tympanum, matching that of the gatehouse. The studded oak folding door to the Hall also deserves attention. It is a fine piece of sixteenth-century craftsmanship and just one of the many carpentry and joinery features that give Cotehele the authentic textures and surfaces of the Tudor period.

The Hall is the showpiece of Cotehele. The upper or dais end is lit by a deep mullioned and transomed granite window, glazed with the usual small panes of leaded glass. On the opposite wall is a massive moulded granite fireplace. The end of the Hall where the lord sat was therefore well served for light and warmth.

High above is the spectacular roof – seven bays of arch-braced trusses, the feet of the principal rafters curving down to the wall in the local cruck tradition. Each bay contains tiers of intersecting

The arch-braced roof of the Hall

wind-braces. Although technically the arch-braces give added support to the trusses and the wind-braces provide longitudinal strength between the trusses, they are moulded and treated decoratively since show was as much a consideration as strength. The basic arch-braced form of the roof is traditional to the South West and survives in houses of a much lower status than Cotehele. It is the quality and richness of the wind-bracing that distinguishes the Cotehele roof from its contemporaries. Only Trecarrel and Wortham, the home of the Dinham family in Lifton parish, west Devon, survive with similar ornamented wind-bracing.

The layout at the lower end of the Hall at Cotehele is unconventional. The end wall contains three service doorways which, in a conventional plan, would lead to the kitchen, pantry and buttery. Here, two now lead into the same room and the third to a passage to the Kitchen and a newel stair.

The Kitchen is offset from the Hall, an unusual position, although not unprecedented and probably a consequence of the geography of the site, which slopes sharply away to the east. This arrangement also had the advantage of allowing reasonable access from the Kitchen, across the service court, to the private rooms in the crosswing by means of the door at the foot of the staircase. More unusual is the direct entry into the body of the Hall. Most hall-houses have a cross-passage between opposing front and back doorways at the lower end, screened off from the main hall. The absence of a screens passage here is probably a product of the relatively late date and perhaps infrequent use of the Hall.

In architectural terms, the Hall at Cotehele is a late example in a long tradition of open halls for which evidence can be found in almost every surviving medieval house. The main distinction between the sixteenth-century Hall at Cotehele and earlier medieval halls is one of usage. In the medieval period the hall was the focus of a communal way of life, often being used not only for eating

The doorway of the south range, with the door to the Hall beyond

and entertaining, but also serving as a kitchen and sleeping quarters as well. By the sixteenth century the lord and his family lived at a greater distance from the other members of their household. As a result, private apartments, set aside for this purpose, became increasingly grand and extensive. This was a general change, lamented as early as the late fourteenth century by the poet William Langland, who recognised that the new remoteness of the master of the house was not merely occasioned by architectural fashion, but had its social consequences for all the members of the household:

Wretched is the hall, each day in the week,
There neither lord nor lady liketh now to sit.
The rich now have a rule to eat by themselves
In a private parlour, in despite of poor men,
Or in a chamber with a chimney, and leave the great hall
That was made for meals, for men to eat in
So that any spilled food was spare for another.

The relationship between the Great Hall and the crosswing, which Sir Piers Edgcumbe added at the west end in the early sixteenth century to contain his private apartments, reveals the increasing emphasis on the privacy of the family in Tudor times. Externally the gable end of the crosswing, facing out over the main court, emulates the grandeur of the Hall, with its ashlar masonry and large mullioned and transomed windows. Internally, the crosswing was conceived on terms of almost equal status with the Hall. Not only were the rooms themselves – the Parlour below (now the Old Dining Room) and the Solar above (now the South and Red Rooms) – of generous size, served by good fireplaces and lit by large windows, but the Solar was given an arch-braced roof with moulded wind-bracing comparable to that of the Hall. (The Solar roof is concealed by a later ceiling and is not on public view.)

The early sixteenth-century programme also included alterations to the south and east ranges. The south range masonry shows that the imposing, crenellated ashlar granite gatehouse has been cut into earlier slatestone rubble. Parallels to the carved granite tympanum, matching that of the Hall door, can be found at Week St Mary Grammar School in north Cornwall, founded in 1506, and at Wor-

tham in Devon. Most of the sixteenth-century internal plan and features of the east range were altered in 1862, when extensive remodelling took place in a style sympathetic to the Tudor character of the building.

Sadly, little evidence has survived of how the house was furnished in Tudor times. We can only fall back on comparative scholarship to imagine a house with a few precious panels of tapestry, perhaps a carpet draped over a table, and a collection of oak bedstocks, tables, forms and stools. There is little of the Tudor period left in the house. Possible survivals are a richly carved armchair in the Hall which may date from the 1590s and a French cabinet of about 1570 on the Lower Landing reminiscent of Du Cerceau's pattern books.

This elaborately carved oak armchair, c.1590, in the Hall is one of the earliest pieces of furniture in the house

CHAPTER THREE

COTEHELE IN THE SEVENTEENTH AND EIGHTEENTH CENTURIES

What kind of household remained at Cotehele in the late sixteenth century after the building of the Mount Edgcumbe house is still a matter of conjecture, as the family records were destroyed during the Second World War. The family may have continued living there, or perhaps it was occupied by dependent relatives, or by a steward carrying out estate administration.

In 1554 Sir Richard Edgcumbe (c.1499–1562) held a splendid party at Mount Edgcumbe for the Admirals of the English, Spanish and Flanders navies, who were in Plymouth preparing for the marriage of Queen Mary and Philip of Spain. Affectionately known as 'the good old man of the castle', he was renowned as a good housekeeper, always ensuring that he had two years of provisions in hand of all things necessary for himself and his family, and keeping £100 in cash for his current needs. In his youth he was interested in astrology and the occult, and in his latter years had to keep a private chaplain to prove his orthodoxy in this troubled period of religious conflict.

His heir, Piers (c.1536–1607/8), was the fourth generation of the family to sit in Parliament and became Sheriff of Devon. He married Margaret Luttrell, a member of another famous West Country family and had nine children. One of these, Margaret, was Queen Elizabeth I's 'own favourite Maid of Honour' and correspondent of Sir Philip Sidney. Satirised as a Puritan in his youth, Piers Edgcumbe was an active MP until his later years when the cost of exploiting the mines on his estate proved a considerable drain on his resources.

(Right) Margaret, Lady Denny, daughter of the Sir Piers Edgcumbe who owned Cotehele in the late sixteenth century. She was the favourite Maid of Honour of Elizabeth I. Painted c.1620 (Plymouth City Museum and Art Gallery, Mount Edgcumbe House Collection)

In 1598 Christopher Harris remarked that 'he goes seldom from his house'.

Sir Piers was succeeded by two of his sons, Piers, and then Sir Richard (c.1570–1638), who was knighted at the Coronation of James I in 1603. By his judicious marriages Sir Richard did much to repair the financial health of the Edgcumbe estates. His first wife, Anne Cary, was described by her sister-in-law as 'a good housewife and very wary in her expenses'. In 1608 he married Mary Coteel, the daughter of Sir Thomas Coteel, a Flemish merchant.

Despite the move to Mount Edgcumbe, Cotehele was added to and improved in the seventeenth century. The first addition, probably in the 1620s, was a suite of rooms arranged in a castellated tower at

Lady Denny's brother, another Piers Edgcumbe, who lived at Cotehele in the early seventeenth century. Painted at the age of 72 (Plymouth City Museum and Art Gallery, Mount Edgcumbe House Collection)

with the north tower and the gateway at the north end of the court.

At the outset of the Civil War in the 1640s, Cotehele was owned by Colonel Piers Edgcumbe (c.1610–67), a Royalist supporter. His home at Mount Edgcumbe was uncomfortably close to the Parliamentarian stronghold of Plymouth and he therefore moved his family and household back to Cotehele for reasons of safety and spent the rest of his life there. The fines he had incurred for his support of the King may have limited his budget for alterations to Cotehele. Nevertheless in the 1650s he replaced the main staircase, which was originally a winding newel stair, with the existing straight flights of timber steps, which necessitated alterations to the existing rooms on the ground floor.

A description of these improvements appears in the earliest building accounts for Cotehele, dated 1651–2. The anonymous builder who was responsible for the work provided plans of the Parlour crosswing with a letter of commentary on the progress and difficulties of the alterations, principally the new 'great stairs'. This is not only full of practical detail, but its tone suggests a patron who

The north-west tower is thought to have been added in the 1620s, perhaps by Sir Thomas Coteel

the north end of Sir Piers's Parlour crosswing. The builder was reputedly Sir Richard Edgcumbe's father-in-law, Sir Thomas Coteel. The tower is an economical piece of planning. It could serve either as a suite of inner retiring rooms beyond the Parlour crosswing or as an independent unit within the Cotehele complex. The increasing demands for privacy and comfort must have led to the need for smaller rooms, and in particular for more bedrooms, and incorporating these into a tower was a sensible way of adding to the building since the rising ground to the north would have made it difficult to extend the house for any length in this direction.

The west range, on the far side of the Retainers' Court, was probably used for the accommodation of servants. Its dating is uncertain because of the plainness of the architectural detail and later alterations to the internal plan. It may be contemporary definitely knew his own mind and kept a close eye on the work:

I know that you do much dislike winding steps, I confess Square ones be better where they can (be) had . . . This is so much as I can express to you in writing . . . but true satisfaction I cannot give you in the particular except you were here of which I have good hope.

The letter gives an insight into the taste of a mid-seventeenth-century owner attempting to refine an earlier dwelling. His desire to provide the crosswing with a more commodious main stair, and another, undated scheme (apparently never executed) for wall panelling are entirely in accordance with the fashion of the time. More unexpected is the information in a further document at the County Record Office in Truro that old windows at Cotehele were being reused and re-sited. Reference is made to a window in the Little Parlour 'that is polled downe and to be converted for a window in the Great Parlour'. The reuse of timber and masonry in new structures had occurred for centuries, but at this date it was certainly not general practice to reuse old

Sir Richard Edgcumbe (1640–88), by Peter Lely (Plymouth City Museum and Art Gallery, Mount Edgcumbe House Collection)

windows in the remodelling of principal rooms. The re-siting of old features and, as the documents show, even the design of new windows with very similar profiles to the old ones, may suggest an appreciation of the value and integrity of the old architecture of the house at a surprisingly early date, but it may simply indicate frugality or lack of money.

After Col. Edgcumbe's death the Edgcumbes spent more time at the modern and comfortable house at Mount Edgcumbe. Col. Edgcumbe's loyalty to the Crown was not forgotten, for his son, Richard (1640–88), was knighted at the Restoration and entertained the King twice at Mount Edgcumbe, in 1671 and 1677. In 1671 he married Lady Anne Montagu, who mysteriously 'died' in 1675, as Richard Polwhele, the historian of Devon and Cornwall relates:

The family were then residing at Cuteel. Lady Edgcumbe had expired: in consequence of what disorder I am not informed. Her body was deposited in the family vault not I suppose in less than a week after her supposed death. The interment, however, had not long taken place, before the sexton, from a motive sufficiently obvious went down into the vault; and observing a gold-ring on her Ladyship's finger, attempted to draw it off; but not succeeding, pressed and pinched the finger – when the body very sensibly moved in the coffin. The man ran off in terror, leaving his lanthorn behind him. Her Ladyship arose, and taking the lanthorn, proceeded to the mansion house. It was about five years after, that of her, Sir Richard was born.

In 1742, this Sir Richard (1680–1758), for many years MP for St Germans and later for Plympton, a Lord of the Treasury, Paymaster-General for Ireland and Chancellor of the Duchy of Lancaster, was created Baron Edgcumbe of Mount Edgcumbe. He was a friend and supporter of the Prime Minister, Sir Robert Walpole, and managed many Cornish pocket boroughs in his interest. At this time the Duchy returned 44 members, whilst there were only 42 for the whole of Scotland, so Edgcumbe's support was worth a good deal. Edgcumbe was raised to the peerage following Walpole's fall from power, in order, their opponents suggested, to avoid an interrogation which might further disgrace the outgoing Prime Minister. He was also a particular favourite of George II, according to some

Richard, later 2nd Baron Edgcumbe, and his younger brother, George, later 1st Earl of Mount Edgcumbe, by Jonathan Richardson, c.1722. Richard displayed artistic ability from an early age, so is shown with a 'porte-crayon', or crayon holder (Plymouth City Museum and Art Gallery, Mount Edgcumbe House Collection)

Richard, 2nd Baron Edgcumbe (again holding a 'porte-crayon') with his friends George Selwyn, standing, and Gilly Williams, behind. Painted by Joshua Reynolds for their mutual friend, Horace Walpole (City of Bristol Museum and Art Gallery)

authorities, because he was even shorter than that diminutive monarch.

John Cornforth has recently suggested that in the 1730s the 1st Baron Edgcumbe may have been responsible for fitting up the principal rooms with the late-seventeenth-century tapestries, more or less in the positions that they occupy today. If this is the case, it is an early example of the revival of ancient interiors that was to become so popular in the late eighteenth and early nineteenth centuries.

Family tradition records that the 1st Baron Edgcumbe was the discoverer of the Plympton-born artist Sir Joshua Reynolds, who as a boy of 12 was on a visit to Mount Edgcumbe:

. . . and on a certain Sunday was at Maker Church with the 1st Lord Edgcumbe and his son. It was noticed that the two boys were misbehaving themselves during the sermon, and when they returned to the house

after the service his Lordship sent for his son, and took him to task for his misconduct. The boy's defence was that Reynolds had drawn such a capital likeness of the vicar on his thumb-nail that they could not stop themselves laughing. The culprit was summoned, and produced the miniature on his nail. After admonishing the young artist with as serious a face as he could command, Lord Edgcumbe ordered him not to wash his hands till the next day, and then giving him a boat house at Cremill [Cremyll] for his studio, a piece of boat-sail for canvas and a few common paints, he set him to make a copy of his first sketch from the life.

Although the story is not authenticated, later in life Joshua Reynolds certainly did paint the 1st Baron Edgcumbe with his dog, of which he was so fond that after its death the skeleton was mounted in the Garden House at Mount Edgcumbe, where he used to go to talk to it.

The 2nd Baron Edgcumbe, his eldest son Richard (1716–61), after a career in the Army also entered Parliament, becoming a Lord of the Admiralty in 1753 and Controller of His Majesty's Household three years later. He was something of an aesthete, a poet and a wit, a friend of George Selwyn, Gilly Williams and Horace Walpole, three of the choicest spirits of the age. He was a friend and patron of Reynolds like his father, and an accomplished draughtsman, as Walpole testifies; his skill 'is said to have been such as might entitle him to a place in the Anecdotes of English Painting, while the ease and harmony of his poetic productions gave him an authorised introduction here'. He was, Walpole goes on to say, 'a man of fine parts, great knowledge and original wit, who possessed a light and easy vein of poetry: who was calculated by nature to serve the public and to charm society'. But, unfortunately, this gifted individual 'was a man of pleasure, and left his gay associates a most affecting example of how health, fame, ambition and everything that may be laudable in principle or practice are drawn into and absorbed by that most destructive of all whirlpools – gaming'. In his youth he gambled away 20 guineas a day at White's, and was only rescued by a political ally, Henry Pelham, who secured for him a secret service pension of £500 a year.

A year after this charming and popular character succeeded to his title in 1758 he received the first royal visitor recorded at Cotehele. *The London Chronicle or Universal Evening Post* of 28–31 July 1759 relates some 'Country News. Saltash July 24 1759 – On Saturday last his Royal Highness Prince Edward [later Duke of York] went up the Tamar from Mount Edgecombe with Lord Edgecombe and several other persons of distinction, in six or eight boats, as far as the water would bear them, towards the Salmon Weir at Calstock. The water failing, horses were procured from the neighbourhood, and his Royal Highness and Lord Edgecumbe rode about a mile from the landing place to the Weir where twenty salmon were caught. A cold collation was conveyed from the Mount to Cothill (the ancient seat of the Edgecomes on the Cornish side of the Tamar) to regale the company on their return.'

Despite fathering four children by his mistress Mrs Ann Franks, the 2nd Baron did not marry her, and so was succeeded as 3rd Baron Edgcumbe by his brother George in 1761. In the same year George married Emma Gilbert, the daughter of the Archbishop of York, and in the following year became a Rear-Admiral. The 3rd Baron Edgcumbe (1720/

1–95) had entered the Navy as a young midshipman, and spent long periods away from Cotehele at sea, seeing much action in the troubled years of the mid-eighteenth century. During the 3rd Baron's spell as Commander-in-Chief in Plymouth (1766–70) the explorer Captain Cook set sail in the *Endeavour* for the South Pacific. It is perhaps in recognition of the 3rd Baron's fine hospitality that Cook named two mountains after him (in New Zealand and Alaska), and an Edgcumbe Bay in Australia.

In 1781 a Royal party visited Mount Edgcumbe and George was created 1st Viscount Mount Edgcumbe and Valletort – some said in recognition of the sacrifice he had made two years earlier by felling many trees in the park at Mount Edgcumbe for the use of the Navy.

On another western progress, in 1789, when George III and Queen Charlotte also visited Cotehele, he was created 1st Earl of Mount Edgcumbe. The Queen has left us a particularly vivid account of this visit:

George, 1st Earl of Mount Edgcumbe, after Joshua Reynolds (Lobby)

... landed at the woods of Cotehill $\frac{1}{2}$ hour after 10 where we found Lrd & Ldy Mount Edgecumbe ready to receive Us. We went in their Coach up to this Old Family seat of theirs where His Ancestors lived at least 200 Years before they had Mount Edgecumbe. It did originally exist of 3 Courts, of which there is now but one existing & Consists of a large Hall full of Old Armor & Swords & Old Carved Chairs of the Times, a Drawing Room Hung with Old Tapestry, the Scirtingboard of which is straw the Chair Seats made of the Priests Vestments. A Chapel which is still in good repair. The Window painted Glass but damaged & defaced. A small Bed Chamber, 2 Closets & a Dressingroom all Hung with Old Tapestry. Above stairs there is a Drawingroom The Chairs Black Ebony Carved & a Cabinet the same, & 4 Bedchambers all Hung the Same. At Breakfast we Eat off the Old Family Pewter, & used Silver knives Forks & Spoons which have been Time immemorial in the Family & have always been kept at this place. The Decanters are of the year 1646 the name of the Wines burnt in the Earthenware for that Time Wines were sold at the Apothecaries Shop & in Sending such a Decanter it was filled with the Wine it bore the Label off. The Desert Plates are Old Delph of a very large Size but make no part of the Old Family Furniture. We embarked again 10 minutes after 12 . . .

Surprisingly for an admiral, the 1st Earl was of both a scientific and an antiquarian mind, being a Fellow of the Royal Society and the Society of Antiquaries, and, like his brother, a friend of Horace Walpole. The 1st Earl shared the family's fascination with Cotehele and its history. He restored Sir Richard Edgcumbe's Chapel in the Wood in 1769, and may have introduced the painting of Sir Richard's tomb at Morlaix now in the Chapel in the house, together with the Gothick blind fretwork on the Chapel screen. John Cornforth has argued that he bought suitably old furniture to increase the romantic appeal at Cotehele. He has also suggested that he acquired the elaborately turned ebony seat furniture in the Drawing Room on which George III and Queen Charlotte sat when they breakfasted at Cotehele. Such furniture, as Clive Wainwright has shown, was avidly sought by members of Walpole's circle, who regarded it, mistakenly, as of Tudor origin. That Cotehele and its contents were exciting widespread interest from the antiquarian-minded by the late eighteenth century is clear from several contemporary references, not least Horace Walpole, who wrote in 1777 with typically jokey exaggeration, 'I never did see Cotehel, and am sorry. Is not the old wardrobe there still? There is one from the time of Cain, but Adam's breeches and Eve's under-petticoat were eaten by a goat in the ark.'

Cotehele's bobbin chairs were the kind of furniture that particularly appealed to Horace Walpole and his circle

CHAPTER FOUR

COTEHELE SINCE 1800

Richard, 2nd Earl of Mount Edgcumbe (1764–1839), was, like his father, a member of the Society of Antiquaries, but seems to have been a less earnest individual – a keen amateur actor, the composer of an opera, *Zenobia*, produced at the King's Theatre, London in 1800, and the author of a much-reprinted account of *Musical Reminiscences of an old Amateur chiefly respecting Italian Opera in England 1773 to 1823* (1825). He was, according to Cyrus Redding, 'a mere fribble, exhibiting little above the calibre of an opera connoisseur, with something of the mimic . . .' He seldom visited Cotehele, except in the summer, when he is said to have lived in an Elizabethan manner. His wife, Lady Sophia Hobart, daughter of the Earl of Buckinghamshire, brought with her a great deal of property at Bere Ferrers on the Devon bank of the Tamar, and much increased the size of the family estate. According to the 4th Earl of Mount Edgcumbe's *Records of the Edgcumbe Family*, 'For many years Cotehele was rarely visited by the family and was left in the care of a farmer and his wife, under whose regime the arms in the hall are said to have received a coat of brown paint every seven years, and the pictures a wash of gin and water every spring and fall'.

The 3rd Earl, Ernest Augustus (1797–1861), was an *aide-de-camp* to Queen Victoria, and received her and Prince Albert at Cotehele during their Western Cruise in 1846. Two years later he was travelling in Europe where he witnessed the revolutions in Palermo and Rome. He published accounts of these journeys and some of the speeches he made in the House of Lords.

In 1840 a Mr Jago, under the pseudonym of the Rev. F. V. J. Arundell, dedicated his account of Cotehele to the 3rd Earl, with lithographs similar to a series of watercolours of Cotehele by the Plymouth artist Nicholas Condy, who signed the Cotehele Visitors' Book in 1836. (The album of watercolours was acquired by Queen Adelaide, wife of William IV, and is now in the Plymouth City Museum.) Mr 'Arundell's' text is heavily laced with the spirit of romantic antiquarianism, as its opening sentences make clear:

It is comparatively but a short time ago when mansion after mansion, possessing even the interest of Cotehele, was suffered to crumble into ruin or taken down to make way for modern erections. Happily that Vandal spirit is arrested, and there is now as eager a search for buildings that have the smallest pretensions to antiquity, and as anxious a desire to save them from further destruction, as there is for every article of furniture, and for every fragment of ancient carved work, which may be supposed to have existed in these mansions of early days.

Ernest Augustus, 3rd Earl of Mount Edgcumbe, by F. Lane after James Sant (Plymouth City Museum and Art Gallery, Mount Edgcumbe House Collection)

Richard, 2nd Earl of Mount Edgcumbe, with his dog, Pepper, by Nicholas Condy (Plymouth City Museum and Art Gallery, Mount Edgcumbe House Collection)

King Charles's Room, c.1840; lithograph by Nicholas Condy

That the author was no furniture historian is revealed by his next, and not unexpected, remark that 'all the rooms retain their ancient furniture, and the latest not more modern than the reign of Elizabeth'. It is with some caution therefore that one approaches the illustrations for the book. Some of the rooms are filled with strange combinations of people – medieval knights and Stuart cavaliers mingling with characters in contemporary dress – and one might suspect that the furniture has been 're-arranged' to accommodate these imaginary figures into convincing compositions. In fact, however, the artist has focused his attention minutely on the rooms themselves and what is inside them, and the rendering of carved woodwork, patterned textiles, even the subject-matter of the tapestries is done with remarkable accuracy and an almost clinical detachment, which gives the rooms a curiously inhospitable appearance. In short, there is little reason to

suppose that the forces of romantic nostalgia have blurred the artist's vision from a faithful record of the appearance of the rooms at that time.

In 1853 the 3rd Earl built a handsome 'marine residence' known as the Winter Villa. This large house stands opposite Mount Edgcumbe and the family would often stay there for a short season when the Fleet was in, or when Assemblies were being held in Plymouth, and thus avoid a possibly rough crossing of the estuary at night.

On his death in 1861 his widow, who was to live for another twenty years, decided that she would like to settle at Cotehele, where no member had lived – other than for short periods – since Col. Piers Edgcumbe had died there in 1660. A major building programme was then put in hand, and Cotehele was awakened from 200 years of comparative slumber. The principal change was in the east wing. This had hitherto consisted on the ground floor of a large butler's pantry, entered from the east end of the Hall, with beer and wine cellars beyond, and on the first floor of servants' bed-chambers ill-lit by

Estate staff in the servants' hall at nearby Mount Edgcumbe, the Edgcumbes' other home; painted by Nicholas Condy (Plymouth City Museum and Art Gallery, Mount Edgcumbe House Collection)

tiny windows. This wing was now to become the living quarters of the dowager Countess.

The work was carried out with unusual respect for the architectural uniformity of the house. A two-storeyed bay was added: the porch on the ground floor, which is dated 1862, became the principal entrance of the house; the window above flooded with light a big new drawing-room on the first floor with a beautiful view down the valley to the Calstock reach of the River Tamar below.

On the ground floor a large dining-room led off the north side of the staircase hall (connected to the original kitchen of the old house), with a library on the south side. Upstairs there were new bedrooms and dressing-rooms. At the north-east angle of the house, where formerly were tumbledown outbuildings and a 'wood hole', a comfortable, two-storey cottage was added for the butler and his wife, now occupied by the National Trust's administrator. The modernisation allowed the Countess to live in centrally heated comfort, though all her rooms still had large open fireplaces.

An album of early photographs of West Country houses includes views of the interior of Cotehele in about 1860, just before the decision to revive the

(Right) The 3rd Earl's wife with their two youngest children, by James Sant. After her husband's death she decided to settle at Cotehele, where the family had not lived permanently since the seventeenth century (Plymouth City Museum and Art Gallery, Mount Edgcumbe House Collection)

(Above) The east front after this wing of the house was converted to living quarters for the dowager Countess in 1862

(Right) William, 4th Earl of Mount Edgcumbe, by Stanhope Forbes (Plymouth City Museum and Art Gallery, Mount Edgcumbe House Collection)

house for contemporary living. These show that although apparently in occupation, the old rooms were still sparsely furnished by the standards of the time, although the arrangements were 'looser' than those recorded by Condy 20 years previously and more cluttered than they appear today. Other photographs taken in the 1870s and '80s serve to show that considerable changes had by then taken place in the arrangement and function of rooms within the core of the old house. Nevertheless, the old rooms remained essentially uncluttered because there appears to have been very little new furniture introduced to supplement the older pieces.

The revival of Cotehele seemed likely to come to an end on the Countess's death, but another similarly happy period was to follow. Her unmarried daughter, Lady Ernestine Edgcumbe, continued to live in the house. She appears to have been something of a tartar, keeping up considerable state, being driven to St Dominick Church, which was much nearer than the parish church of Calstock, in a carriage with cockaded footmen. The old servants who were still at Cotehele when the National Trust acquired it in 1947 remembered her well. Lady Ernestine lived at Cotehele for over 20 years, moving in about 1905 to live at Honeycombe, another house belonging to the family, next to Buddles Adit – where she had 'first pull' on the Cotehele water supply. She lived at Honeycombe until her death in 1925.

Her brother, William Henry, 4th Earl of Edgcumbe (1832–1917), was a considerable figure in the county. Much preferring Cornwall to London he was a good landlord, taking pleasure in the management of the extensive Edgcumbe estates.

With Lord St Levan of St Michael's Mount, he was the owner of the toll bridge ('the Halfpenny Bridge') which connected Plymouth to Devonport and brought in a handsome revenue every year. Travellers, however, found this a great burden, as every foot passenger, except for soldiers, had to pay the toll. This was particularly resented by the many sailors in the port, where from at least 1850 it is recorded that after mess they sang the following song:

Lordy Edgcumbe, Lord divine
All the Hakey fish are thine;
All the fishes in the sea
Noble Lord belong to thee.

Lordy Edgcumbe, we are told
That you've bags and bags of gold;
So lift the Toll, for this is true,
What's much for us is nought for you.

Lordy Edgcumbe, up the hill,
'Tis a shame to treat us ill;
Marines and soldiers go through free,
Then why the b————h——— can't we?

As well as being Lord Lieutenant of Cornwall and holding many active or honorary offices, the 4th Earl was the first Chairman of the County Council, from 1898 until his death in 1917, and President of the Council for the building of Truro

Piers, 5th Earl of Mount Edgcumbe, at Cotehele

Cathedral. He was a friend of the Prince of Wales, and accompanied him on his trips abroad. He was also Lord Chamberlain in 1879–80 and Lord Steward in 1885–6. His first wife, Lady Katherine Hamilton, daughter of the Duke of Abercorn, died in 1874, and 32 years later he married his cousin, Caroline Cecilia, previously the Countess of Ravensworth.

The 4th Earl was his family's historian and put in order and then catalogued the enormous number of family muniments (sadly destroyed when Mount Edgcumbe was bombed in 1941). He published his *Records of the Edgcumbe Family* in 1888, which are an invaluable source for the history of Cotehele.

He was succeeded as 5th Earl by his son, Piers (1865–1944), who served in the Boer War and then busied himself with local affairs, though on a lesser scale than his father had done. He was widowed in 1935, and having been bombed out of Mount Edgcumbe, he came to live at Cotehele. His obitu-

The 6th Earl and Countess of Mount Edgcumbe in their coronation robes, by Mills, 1935 (Plymouth City Museum and Art Gallery, Mount Edgcumbe House Collection)

ary in the local paper after his death in 1944 conjured up a vivid picture of those troubled years:

So Passes a Bit of England . . . The Fifth Earl of Mount Edgcumbe was one of the old-fashioned earls – old-fashioned in the best sense . . . But war, and the death of the master has broken up the big household just as it has done many another. . . The London house in Belgrave Square has been closed since early in the war. . . The pleasure gardens of the estate in Cornwall are taken over by the military. . . The yacht has been laid up since the war. . . The kitchen garden is producing food which is marketed. . . The woodmen are carrying out their work for the Government.

His cousin, Kenelm Edgcumbe (1873–1965), became 6th Earl. He was an eminent electrical engineer, the founder of the Everett Edgcumbe Company in 1900, and in 1927 President of the Institute of Electrical Engineers. Tragically, he had lost his only son, Piers, in action in Holland in May 1940, but he was determined to play his part in the restoration of his family home. He and his wife came to live at Cotehele while a house was being converted for them in the stables at Mount Edgcumbe. Thenceforward he devoted himself to the rebuilding of the main house, completing it in 1960 at the age of 87.

Upon succeeding to the family estate, he had suggested to the Treasury that the Cotehele property of 1,300 acres should be accepted in part payment of death duties, and handed over to the National Trust. This was done in 1947, and thus Cotehele became the first historic house and estate to be acquired by the Trust through this mechanism. The Trust is deeply indebted both to the Treasury and to the 6th Earl of Mount Edgcumbe whose persistence and patient negotiation established an invaluable precedent. He died in 1965 and the family trustees generously continued to leave on loan in the state rooms all the tapestries, armour and furniture. In 1974 most of these contents were, in their turn, given to the Trust by the Treasury which had accepted them in lieu of estate duty on the death of the 6th Earl.

Edward Piers Edgcumbe, a distant cousin from New Zealand, succeeded as 7th Earl in 1965 and divided his time between Mount Edgcumbe and his sheep farm in the Antipodes. His nephew, Robert Charles, is the present and 8th Earl of Mount Edgcumbe. He has five daughters and also spends part of the year in Britain and part in New Zealand.

CHAPTER FIVE

THE TAPESTRIES

To the exclusion of all other hangings, the walls of Cotehele are covered with tapestry. This is unusual. Most of these tapestries date from the later seventeenth century; and this too is rather strange, given the taste of the time for conspicuous variety in wall-coverings. Not for Cotehele, apparently, the silk damask, mohair, camlet, velvet and cloth-of-gold of Ham House, nor the gilt leather, clouded silk, calico, painted satin, striped plush, cheyney and plaid of Dyrham Park. By the end of the century Ham, a miniature palace furnished with no expense spared by the Lauderdales, had only five sets of tapestry; Dyrham, newly built by William Blathwayt with his wife's fortune, had only three sets; yet at Cotehele there are the remains of some eighteen sets of tapestry hangings, at least fourteen dating from between 1650 and 1700, with detached borders suggesting that once there were more. Yet more pieces, now lost, are illustrated in a nineteenth-century book on the house. When this impressive collection was assembled is uncertain.

There is no difficulty in imagining the earlier tapestries as part of Edgcumbe family history. In the Old Dining Room and the Punch Room are odd borders to which have been added rectangles of tapestry displaying a boar's head, an element in Edgcumbe heraldry. A verdure in Queen Anne's Room is of a date to have belonged to Sir Piers Edgcumbe (1468/9–1539), under whom the main building of Cotehele was completed. Two upright borders in the Old Dining Room, with plants twining round a thick palm-tree stem bearing birds and clusters of fruit, were designed in the second quarter of the sixteenth century and could have come from tapestries furnishing either Cotehele or Mount Edgcumbe, built in 1553.

Similarly the late sixteenth- and early seventeenth-century tapestries are too few to present a problem. Though the baroque allegory of *The Story of Mankind* dating from the 1630s is too tall for the room it now occupies, these Brussels tapestries and the Dutch tapestry of *Iphigenia* could have been bought following the addition to Cotehele of the tower built in the 1620s by Sir Thomas Coteel, a merchant trading with the Netherlands. The *Iphigenia* series, however, dates from around 1650, and it is doubtful whether Sir Thomas was then still alive.

His grandson, Col. Piers Edgcumbe, who died in 1667, was the only head of the family thought to have lived at Cotehele in the seventeenth century. He might reasonably be expected to have taken an active interest in furnishing the house. Some of the Flemish pieces of the 1660s could have been bought by him through former contacts of Sir Thomas. Being a royalist, however, defeat in the Civil War meant financial loss. When the Restoration, in 1660, brought abortive plans for a loyalist Order of the Royal Oak, his income was assessed at £2,000 a year – respectable wealth in those days, but hardly in the income bracket for buying more than the occasional set of tapestry. None of the pieces at Cotehele is woven with gold and silver thread, which could have sent the price over £8 the Flemish ell (an area of weaving 27 × 27 inches); but they do contain a fair amount of silk and many large-scale, finely woven figures. As a prospective purchaser was warned in 1670, tapestries 'full of figures, faces and nakeds wilbe deare'. An average set of tapestry of the time might contain 120 to 170 ells at around £2 to £3 the ell.

When the son of Piers, another Richard, died in 1688, he bequeathed £4,000 to each of his three daughters, indicating improvement in the family fortunes. He lived at Mount Edgcumbe, and it is likely that some of the tapestries of his time were purchased for that house but moved to Cotehele later, as they became unfashionable. That would

The Old Dining Room, c.1840, lithograph by Nicholas Condy; showing the Picus fragment and the Verdures in position as now, but without added borders

account in part for the drastic alterations made to fit them to the rooms there. A letter to Sir Richard Edgcumbe dated 1673 shows he had by then bought at least one set of tapestries. Geerardt van Heythuysen, a merchant living in London who traded with Antwerp, where so many of the tapestries at Cotehele were produced, wrote: 'I think I have some small aquaintance in selling a Suite of Tapissry hangings to your selfe'. Antwerp records of the firm Wauters, Cockx and de Wael in the 1680s name the tapestry series exported to this merchant in London, including sets of *Children's Games* and *Verdures*. Perhaps the *Children's Games* in the Red Room, with the mark of Philippus Wauters, were acquired by Sir Richard.

Still lacking, however, is any evidence of purchasing activity in the 1660s to 1680s on a scale needed to assemble the 35 tapestries of that time at Cotehele surviving from twelve sets, two of them duplicates, that once might have comprised well over seventy pieces. Sir Richard was succeeded by a minor, so even those series that remained popular in the 1690s are more likely to have been acquired, if bought new for the family, before his death in 1688. Might the strange circumstances of the tapestries at Cotehele be better explained if some of the hangings there had been second-hand purchases in the eighteenth century by an Edgcumbe with antiquarian interests? This would make sense of the exclusive use of tapestry, the arbitrary way in which the pieces are cut and joined to fit rooms for which they were not originally made, and of the placing of tapestry across doorways, with odd borders filling every gap on the walls, over fireplaces, above doors and under windows, in a spurious attempt to impart a 'medieval' character to the furnishings.

That such an exercise occurred was implied in

*The Red Room, c.1840, lithograph by Nicholas Condy;
showing the 'Children's Games' in their present positions,
with the piece to the left of the door augmented by a fragment
of 'Romulus and Remus', but with a fragment of 'The
Bacchanals', now in the Punch Room, over the fireplace*

1814 in the volume on Cornwall of *Magna Britannia*
by Daniel and Samuel Lysons: 'Cotehele House,
which retains its ancient form, has been fitted up
with furniture corresponding to its appearance'.
John Cornforth's articles in *Country Life* (1990) support this theory; and the account there quoted of
Queen Charlotte's visit to Cotehele, in which she
mentioned nine rooms 'all hung with Old
Tapestry', suggests that the transformation may
already have taken place by 1789. Cornforth con-
siders this installation to be the work of the 1st
Baron Edgcumbe in the 1730s or '40s, but the dis-
tinctly Romantic approach to the medieval, seen in
the way the hangings are used, seems more likely
at a slightly later date. The Baron Edgcumbe who

died in 1761 was a man of artistic talents, while the
brother who succeeded him was an antiquarian.
Both were friends of that advocate of the Gothick
style, Horace Walpole.

In the absence of inventories of the Edgcumbe
houses detailing the tapestries and where they hung;
or of family bills or accounts that might have shown
when tapestry was purchased; or of more informa-
tive letters or diaries describing acquisition or installation, the question of when this large collection of
later seventeenth-century tapestry was made is
likely to remain unsolved. All we know for certain
is that most of the pieces now at Cotehele were there
by about 1840, when tapestries from eleven sets
were described in a *History of Cotehele* by the 'Rev.
F. V. J. Arundell', illustrated by Nicholas Condy.
The book is invaluable. It shows that some alterations to the hangings had already taken place, particularly cutting pieces to fit over fireplaces, and that
some tapestries even then hung in their present loca-
tions, as in the Old Dining Room and partly in the

35

Red Room. The book also shows, however, many tapestries differently arranged, and some that have since been lost. It reminds us that the contents of a house were frequently altered and rearranged, warning against assumptions about historic furnishings from what we see today.

THE TAPESTRIES AND THEIR MAKERS

Throughout the sixteenth and seventeenth centuries, Europe was chiefly supplied with tapestry from the workshops of the southern Netherlands: Brussels, the capital, tended to produce the richest tapestry; Antwerp, Bruges and Enghien made excellent middle quality pieces and some coarser; Oudenaarde produced the cheapest and coarsest. Because tapestry was highly prized during these centuries, they had an immense export industry. Rulers of other countries tried to set up their own workshops to reduce the drain on their economies, amongst them James I who established a manufactory at Mortlake in 1619. In the second half of the century Mortlake lost its monopoly, and several independent workshops were encouraged by the Crown, particularly that owned by the current Yeoman Arrasworker, who was responsible for the repair of tapestries in the royal collection. When Mortlake ceased production and closed in 1703, smaller establishments remained to keep the art alive in England through much of the eighteenth century.

However many tapestries were made in England they were insufficient to satisfy demand. Much tapestry was imported. The Antwerp merchants even had pieces of specially low height woven for the English market, to hang above the wainscot, as was the fashion here, like the *Pygmalion* tapestry (White Room). Of all the tapestries at Cotehele, only two or three sets can be identified as English, one is Dutch, and all the rest are Flemish, with some six or seven Antwerp series dating from the 1660s to the 1680s. Identification is sometimes difficult in that enterprising English tapestry-makers cut costs by copying successful imports.

With the exceptions of pirated copies and those rare occasions when sets were specially commissioned and the design bought by the customers to keep their tapestries exclusive, the designs and cartoons (full-scale paintings from which the weavers worked) usually remained the property of the tapestry-maker and would continue in production as long as the series would sell. The tapestry-maker was the man whose name or mark was woven into the tapestry. He might be either the owner of a tapestry workshop or a merchant financing the weaving and owning the cartoons, in which case the same designs might be woven by different workshops. The actual weavers were not often recorded by name. Six or more might work together on a tapestry: the most skilful weaving the faces, naked flesh and intricate details, the others filling in the plainer draperies and backgrounds.

Tapestry-making was often a family business. Several of the Antwerp series at Cotehele come from ramifications of one family: the *Caesar Augustus* and *Numa Pompilius* tapestries (White Room, South Room) are from the workshop of Jan Frans Cornelissen, brother-in-law to Philippus and Michiel Wauters. Philippus Wauters supplied the *Children's Games* (Red Room): Michiel Wauters, a merchant dealing in tapestry, lace and cloth, owned the cartoons of *The Liberal Arts* (White Room, Red Room, Upper Landing, King Charles's Room). All three men were dead by 1680, Michiel Wauters's business being left to his daughters and their husbands, with his eldest daughter, Maria-Anna Wauters de Thisius, in charge. She continued to supply the series provided earlier by her father and uncles, and conducted a brisk trade in tapestries of *The Story of Circe* (Old Dining Room, Red Room, King Charles's Room).

The Wauters's London agent, Geerardt van Heythuysen, lived in the parish of St. Peter the Poor from at least 1646, when he was married in the Dutch Church of Austin Friars, to his death in 1693. He was buried in the same church, as was his widow a year later. His only child having died of the plague in 1665, he was succeeded in the business by a nephew of the same name born in England.

THE TAPESTRIES TODAY

It may be difficult for the visitor to Cotehele to imagine the tapestries as they once were. Sets of related subjects are scattered through the house. Some pieces have been arbitrarily cut in two, so that Circe and Picus, who should be looking at each other, are isolated over fireplaces in different rooms, and the admiring neighbours of Romulus and Remus are sewn to a tapestry of naked children playing with marbles. Other tapestries have been reduced to pitiful fragments, like the truncated figures cut from *Circe* subjects that should have been up to 18 ft wide, with ornate buildings set in perspective vistas of formal gardens (King Charles's Room). Borders have been removed from the sets to which they belong and applied to others, confusing their identity.

Worse than this, tapestries tend to become mere ghosts of their former beauty through colours fading where they have been subjected to too much light. Greens have turned blue, their fugitive yellows lost, blue skies have muted to grey or neutral shades, reds have become brown and flesh tones changed to an unhealthy putty colour. The backs of the tapestries still show the original vibrant greens and sun-tanned flesh tones. Some tapestries at Cotehele have fortunately been protected in dark rooms or shielded by beds, like *Geometry*, the tapestry now on the Upper Landing, and the *Verdures* in the Old Dining Room. Recently washed, these still make their original impact on the beholder.

The National Trust is actively involved in a long programme of tapestry conservation, necessitating the occasional removal of tapestries from Cotehele so that the dirt obscuring their colours can be removed and their fabric strengthened.

THE OLD DINING ROOM

Orpheus and Eurydice
Antwerp; around 1700

The first tapestry one sees, to the right on entering, is the youngest in the house, from *c.* 1700. Ostensibly a landscape with nymphs gathered by a foun-tain, the most important scene is hidden: where the tapestry is caught up at one corner to allow access to the Punch Room, a section shows Eurydice, kneeling, poisoned by a snake biting her heel. Her husband, Orpheus, whose singing and playing on the lyre charmed wild beasts and even trees and stones, followed his dead wife into the Underworld. By his music, he moved the rulers of the Afterlife to reprieve Eurydice, who would live if Orpheus could lead her back to the world above without looking at her. At the last moment he turned and looked back, so losing Eurydice again until he died, killed by the women of Thrace because he would take no other wife.

This tapestry is the only one of the set to survive at Cotehele, but other episodes – Orpheus turning to look at Eurydice, and his own death – are found elsewhere in the same elaborate floral border with heads of fox, spaniel, lion and monkey. *The Killing of Orpheus* is signed by the tapestry-maker 'I. VAN DER GOTEN'. As 'I' stood for 'J', this was probably Jacob van der Goten who worked in Antwerp until 1720. Remains of the woven name 'I. VAN DER . . .' can be seen in the Punch Room arbitrarily sewn to a different tapestry. Fortunately the Rev. F. V. J. Arundell recorded the complete name, I. van der

Eurydice poisoned by a snake, hidden by a door flap, in a single surviving tapestry from an 'Orpheus and Eurydice' series (Old Dining Room)

Goten, so the identification of the Cotehele set is confirmed. What has become of the other *Orpheus* tapestries once here no one knows. Only the borders remain, used to lengthen the *Verdures* in this room at some time after Condy drew it in the late 1830s, if the illustration is accurate.

Verdures
Antwerp; last quarter seventeenth century

Landscapes or 'verdure' tapestries, bringing the fresh greens of parks and woodlands into often ill-lit, gloomy interiors, and extending confined surroundings by glimpses of distant prospects, were always popular. If these tapestries were here when the room was used for dining, the diners could have imagined themselves 'al fresco' in the pastoral setting. There is no discernible story linking these woodland scenes: the twins, Diana, with a crescent moon in her hair, and Apollo, his head encircled by the rays of the sun, carry bows and arrows as though to hunt; women hold a wreath for a goat to jump through; couples dance in abandon to rustic music. Apollo, as well as being the sun god, was the deity of shepherds in ancient mythology, but the designer may have intended no such theme. Many sets of tapestry of this period were known simply as 'verdures with little figures'. Narrow borders and tiny figures, needing less skill in weaving, make these the least expensive tapestries in the room.

The Story of Circe
Antwerp; probably 1680s

Over the fireplace is part of a tapestry halfway in quality between the *Verdures* and the *Orpheus* tapestry. It shows the young King Picus out hunting, riding a spirited horse and carrying two spears, as described in Ovid's *Metamorphoses*. He is about to be transformed into a woodpecker by the enchantress Circe for refusing to become her lover. The figure of Circe from this tapestry, gazing at Picus, is over the fireplace in the Red Room.

A story within a story in Ovid, the tale of Picus is told by one of Circe's attendants to a follower of Ulysses after Ulysses had rescued his men, themselves transformed into animals by Circe's magic. At least three of seven possible *Story of Circe* subjects

were once at Cotehele; for two very small fragments showing men in armour from scenes with Ulysses and Circe are to be seen in King Charles's Room. English purchasers appreciated the charm of this series. At least sixteen sets were recorded as exported to England between 1682 and 1698 by the Antwerp firm of Wauters, Cockx and de Wael. Their records also give the names of the artists: Pieter Ykens for the figures and Pieter Spierinckx for the landscapes.

The odd borders in this room have been discussed in the section on the Edgcumbe family.

THE PUNCH ROOM

The Bacchanals
English; 1670s–1680s

In Condy's time this room, called the Ante-Room, contained tapestries of the Liberal Arts, with Circe over the mantelpiece. Some of the tapestries now cut and pieced to fit this room were, however, at Cotehele around 1840, a 'Vintage' being mentioned by Arundell in Queen Anne's Room, and the Bacchic procession over the fireplace here, illustrated by Condy already cut to fit the fireplace in the Red Room. The two fireplace pieces have since been transposed. Other versions of this series have the procession, with a boy Bacchus riding a goat, forming the right side of a much larger tapestry; in the centre are the boy fauns or satyrs (here on the window wall) who, dancing, lead the procession towards a group at the left (here by the door) where a boy up a tree is peeing, to the alarm of a little girl below. The sensibilities of later owners being offended by this scene, it was often amended by reweaving or patching, as here. Another alteration in this room may be seen on the wall opposite the window, where a vintage scene has been arbitrarily joined to a separate tapestry showing a goat startled by a boy with a mask. They were in place by 1907 when they were photographed by Charles Latham for *In English Homes*.

The goat was sacred to Bacchus, so fauns and satyrs, half-goat, half-human, were his followers, assisting with the vintage and subsequent revels. Two identical grape-treading scenes here, one in a

Treading grapes: from 'The Bacchanals' (Punch Room)

bead-and-reel border, one with flowers and scrolling leaves, suggest that the Edgcumbes owned two sets of this attractive series. The themes of Bacchanalian revels and children at play, both highly popular in the seventeenth century, are here combined in a series which may have been known as *The Bacchanals*. This name was used at the end of the century to describe a set from these same designs at Boughton House in Northamptonshire in a distinctive border used on tapestries signed by Francis Poyntz; Thomas Poyntz, a London tapestry-maker in the 1680s, signed adapted versions of these same designs in a leaf-and-flower border like the one at Cotehele; and Francis Poyntz, Yeoman Arras-worker, in 1667–8 made for Charles II 'Hangings called the Bacchinalls . . . being the first after the Designe'. Though the tapestries here are English,

either by Poyntz or from Mortlake (there is a Mortlake mark on the peeing scene), the designs probably came from abroad since the palatial gardens with elaborate parterres, topiary work and fountains are close to those in Flemish tapestries.

THE WHITE ROOM

The Bacchanals

At the right of the entrance is another tapestry of *The Bacchanals*, much cut about and pieced. It shows children teasing one of their companions near a huge fountain, itself a life-sized sculpture of Bacchanalian children. All the rest comes from cannibalised tapestries. The boy in the centre, stick in raised hand, is from another scene with the startled goat like that in the Punch Room: the fountain top at the right is the same in reverse as the one on the

Venus gives Phaon youth and beauty: from a series of stories after Ovid (White Room)

left, the reversal indicating copying, possibly by a different workshop. The border comes from another tapestry.

Pygmalion
Antwerp or London; 1670s–1690s

Two other tapestries in this room are all that remains at Cotehele of a set that might have had as many as eleven mythological subjects from various stories. Still whole, though cut for doors to open, the long piece over the wainscot between entrance and window tells the story of Pygmalion. He was a sculptor who made such a beautiful statue of a woman that he fell in love with it and prayed to Venus, seen here in the sky in her chariot drawn by swans, that the statue might become human. His prayer was granted. The designer has included another figure, the goddess Minerva, watching the sculptor at work. Possibly the designer confused Pygmalion with another figure from myth, Prometheus who, according to one creation legend, made statues of mankind and gave them life helped by Minerva.

Venus and Phaon
Antwerp or London; 1670s–1690s

From the same set is a tapestry cut in two: a frag-ment with a boat over the door, and, over the fire-place, a panel with Venus, Cupid and a young-looking man. He is Phaon, formerly an elderly boatman who took pity on a poor old woman and rowed her across the sea without payment. Once on shore she revealed herself as Venus in disguise and bestowed on him youth and beauty, the notion of the gift represented by Venus handing him a box. The Antwerp tapestries in this series were so pop-ular in England that an English workshop copied them. The Cotehele scenes are woven in the same direction as some English pieces.

Caesar Augustus
Antwerp; 1660s–1670s

The tapestry behind the crewel-work bed is from yet another Antwerp series. In the borders are the shortened words 'VIC. AUG., PAX AUG.', indicating the Victories and Peace of Augustus, successor to his uncle Julius Caesar and the first Emperor of Rome. What remains of the tapestry shows a modestly deprecating Caesar Augustus who should be accepting the kneeling homage of Tiberius Nero in the middle of the latter's triumphal progress, but in the Cotehele tapestry these figures are missing. Another mutilated fragment from this series hangs in the South Room.

The Liberal Arts
Antwerp; 1660s–1670s

Next to the *Phaon* tapestry is a fragment with a cock heralding the rising sun, while a torch symbolic of departing night is held by Atlas, supporter of the heavens, who carries a celestial globe on his shoulders. Most of his figure and the whole of a woman personifying Astronomy are missing from this tapestry, which comes from a documented Antwerp series of the seven *Liberal Arts*. The cartoons, designed by Daniel Janssens (died 1682), were noted in the inventory of Michiel Wauters taken on his death in 1679.

Condy's illustration of the White Room shows that *Astronomy* had been cut to fit its present position before 1840. His view of the Ante-Room (now called the Punch Room) is even more useful, showing on the fireplace wall a lost tapestry of *Rhetoric* cut in two. Rhetoric stands on a rostrum addressing a group of men, some of whom are at the far right of the fireplace wall in the illustration. She holds the caduceus, a wand entwined with snakes and topped by wings, which was an attribute of Mercury, messenger and herald of the gods, and so symbolic of eloquence. On the steps by her is a caged parrot, the only part of this tapestry to survive at Cotehele, now forming one of two flaps added to the tapestry of *Grammar* in King Charles's Room. *Logic* and *Music* are missing from the Cotehele *Liberal Arts*. *Geometry*, *Grammar* and *Arithmetic* all survive intact, *Arithmetic* in two versions, which, with the two types of border found on these pieces, suggests that the Edgcumbes owned two sets of this series. An eighth subject in the series, showing all seven Liberal Arts together, hangs in the Red Room, partly hidden by the bed. It was also illustrated by Condy in the Ante-Room. From left to right the Arts and

(Below) The Ante-Room (now the Punch Room), c.1840, lithograph by Nicholas Condy. The room then contained tapestries of 'The Liberal Arts', including a now lost tapestry of 'Rhetoric'. 'Circe', over the fireplace, is now in the Red Room

'Geometry' from
'The Liberal Arts'
(Upper Landing)

their attributes are: Astronomy, winged, her head encircled by stars; Logic, seated, a snake twined round her arm; Grammar and Arithmetic, walking together, holding a scroll with the alphabet and a slate with calculations; Rhetoric, with caduceus and parrot; Geometry, in a large, rayed hat, with a terrestrial globe; and Music, playing an instrument in the background.

THE UPPER LANDING

The Liberal Arts
Antwerp; 1660s–1670s

The individual tapestry for Geometry represents her, still wearing her distinctive hat, holding a pair of dividers over a terrestrial globe. The man with the measuring stick is probably meant to be the great geometrician Euclid.

THE RED ROOM

Children's Games
Antwerp; 1660s–1670s

This room is dominated by a set of tapestries which now seems rather drab, but which when new would have appeared fresh with innumerable greens in the foliage and delicate pink shades in the flesh of the naked children absorbed in their games. These may originally have been considered suitable tapestries for the bedchamber of the lady of the house, leaving the Roman histories, with their battles and bloodshed, for the gentleman's chambers. Altered to hang in their present positions, the piece with children playing marbles has joined to it, at the left, the left side of *Children bowling hoops*, and, at the right, a strip in contrasting style cut from *Romulus and Remus distributing the brigands' loot* (South Room). Condy's illustration shows this alteration was done before about 1840.

To the left of the fireplace, over which is the tapestry of *Circe*, the original floral border of *Chil-*

dren's Games displays the mark incorporating the initials 'PW' of the tapestry-maker Philippus Wauters of Antwerp. His tapestries were exported all over Europe. In 1676 he offered to sell to dealers in Vienna 'Children's games in landscapes with views and prospects, the children drawn by van Diepenbeeck as large as life', tapestries likely to be from the same cartoons as the set at Cotehele. Though drawn for the tapestries by Abraham van Diepenbeek, the figures of the children are based on works by Jacques Stella published as engravings in 1657.

Romulus and Remus
Brussels; 1660s

Behind the entrance door is the first complete tapestry of *Romulus and Remus* or *The Foundation of Rome*. Five subjects from the series are divided

(Above) Children bowling hoops; detail from 'Children's Games' (Red Room)

(Right) Inscription and part of a battle scene; detail from the 'Romulus and Remus' series (Red Room)

between this room, the South Room and the Drawing Room. As told by Livy, the story is that
Numitor was deposed by his brother Amulius, who
forced Numitor's only child, Rhea Sylvia, to
become a Vestal Virgin so that there should be no
heirs. When Rhea Sylvia nevertheless had twin
boys, whom she said were the sons of the god Mars,
the infants were left exposed to die, but were suc-
kled by a she-wolf and found by a shepherd. The
children grew up as his, distinguishing themselves
by their bravery, taking the spoils of robbers and
giving them to the local peasants. Romulus and
Remus were eventually identified, killed Amulius
and restored their grandfather (whom Amulius had
unaccountably neglected to kill) to the throne of
Alba. Numitor gave them land of their own on
which they founded a city named after whoever
saw the more auspicious augury in the flight of
birds. Remus first saw six vultures; but Romulus
then saw twelve birds: so both claimed the greater
success. In the dispute which followed, Romulus
killed Remus and gave Rome his own name. As his
followers were all male, he invited his neighbours
the Sabines to celebrations, at which he seized their
women. Later, to prevent bloodshed, the women
reconciled their fathers and brothers with their new
husbands.

The battle scene in this room shows by its inscription that the small group of figures scanning the
sky in the distance at the left is watching for the
augury. Town mark and maker's name are woven
at the bottom edge. The two 'Bs' stand for Brussels
and Brabant, where the tapestry-maker Jan van
Rottom was active in the 1660s. In the highly
organised Flemish manufactories of this period, two
or more workshops would often contract to produce one set of tapestries to meet demand more
quickly. This series was woven in the workshops
of both Jan van Rottom and Erasmus de Pan-
nemaker, whose initials are on a piece in the next
room. The designs are based on tapestries of the sixteenth century; this battle, incongruously, is taken
from a tapestry of the young Scipio rescuing his
father at the Battle of the Ticino.

THE SOUTH ROOM

Romulus and Remus
Brussels; 1660s

Immediately to the left of the entrance is the
tapestry of *The Rape of the Sabines* with Pan-
nemaker's initials. The central couple in the tapestry
are Romulus, with close-cropped hair and dressed
in scale armour, and his bride-to-be Hersilia. The
older couple to the left are sometimes found as a
separate tapestry, in which they represent Mars and
Rhea Sylvia, the parents of Romulus; here they are
just additional figures to make a wider *Rape of the
Sabines*. Looped back over the archway into the
Hall squint is a much cut and patched tapestry of
the twins dividing the robbers' booty: to the left
of the bed, *The Building of Rome*, the twins directing
operations from under an awning at the right.

Caesar Augustus
Antwerp; 1660s–1670s

Set over the fireplace among the Romulus and
Remus tapestries is the second fragment of the
Caesar Augustus series, a sacrifice by the pious
Emperor on an altar inscribed in Latin 'To the
Unknown God'. Christians found this sacrifice significant in that Christ was born during the reign
of Augustus. The series, in eight pieces, was first
woven in the Antwerp workshop of Jan Frans Cornelissen (died 1678), the cartoons passing to his
brother-in-law, Michiel Wauters (died 1679), and
so to the latter's daughter, Maria-Anna. The
borders on the other fragment in the White Room
suggest these pieces date from the 1660s or 1670s.

Numa Pompilius
Antwerp; 1660s–1670s

The magnificent tapestry between bed and entrance
door was also woven in Jan Frans Cornelissen's
workshop. From its border, it too probably dated
from the 1660s or 1670s, though Cornelissen's niece
was selling both *Caesar Augustus* and *Numa
Pompilius* tapestries in the 1680s. Numa Pompilius,
next ruler of Rome after Romulus, is portrayed
wearing a striped turban and crown. He is accompanied by priests in white robes, and by lictors
carrying the bundle of rods bound with an axe, the

Numa Pompilius closing the Temple of Janus : detail (South Room)

symbol of authority in Rome. Numa instituted laws and customs, regulated religious observances, reformed the calendar and built the Temple of Janus, which was to be open in time of war and closed in time of peace. The Romans being a war-like nation, it was rarely shut. Here Numa points with his sceptre to the men conveying military trophies and weapons of war to be deposited in the temple at the left of the tapestry. There were six subjects in the complete series: but no clue as to how many were in the set at Cotehele.

A lost tapestry

During the late 1830s and early 1840s, when this room was known as the Best Bedroom, the *History of Cotehele* showed a tapestry here that now is missing. The Rev. Arundell described it as 'representing dogs of different descriptions, admirably done, evidently designed by Snyders and Rubens'. Condy illustrated only a distinctive border, a column with crossed spears, the bottom part obscured by a portion of a figure protruding from the picture space. These indications are sufficient to identify the lost tapestry as a hunter and his dogs from tapestries of *Country Life*, designed not by Rubens but by another artist of the Baroque, Jacob Jordaens. His original drawing of around 1635 for this tapestry is in the Victoria and Albert Museum, and a fine tapestry in a similar border is in the Vienna State Collection.

THE OLD DRAWING ROOM

The Story of Mankind
Brussels; 1630s

Apart from the fragment over the fireplace, *Romulus and Remus before Numitor*, all the tapestries in this room are from one series in six subjects, a rather laboured baroque allegory known as *The Story of Mankind*. The designs are attributed to the Flemish artist Anthonie Sallaert, and the tapestries were woven by the workshop of Hendrick Reydams in Brussels. In the first of four subjects here, the pagan gods Jupiter, Minerva and Diana of the Ephesians and the Virtue, Temperance, distinguished by the restraining bridle which is her

Time drives away the Pleasures, from 'The Story of Mankind' (Old Drawing Room)

attribute, strive to influence Mankind. The next two pieces have been made smaller than the original cartoons, cutting off figures vital to the story. Ceres, Bacchus and Venus should be seen tempting youthful Mankind to pleasures while Cupid drives away Temperance. Time then drives away the Pleasures, leaving aged Man attended by Temperance and Prudence. The finale is a vast *Triumph of Virtue*. She rides in a chariot drawn by the four Cardinal Virtues, represented as four winged boys holding their attributes: Justice, scales and a sword; Prudence, a mirror and a snake; Fortitude, carrying a column on his shoulder; and Temperance, with bridle and a glass innocent of wine. They trample the fallen figures of Time, Death, Envy (gnawing on a human heart), Diana of the Ephesians and blindfolded Fortune. The three Theological Virtues – Faith, Hope and Charity, with cross, anchor and blazing heart – hold the symbol of Eternity above the head of Virtue, while four winds blow flowers around the cortège which is flanked by four laurel-wreathed philosophers seated on clouds.

QUEEN ANNE'S ROOM

Verdure with flowers and animals
Flemish; early sixteenth century

On the entrance wall is the earliest hanging at Cotehele, unhappily cut to accommodate the arch of the door. The tapestry is filled with large flowering plants, mostly drawn from nature but including wild roses slightly stylised, like heraldic Tudor roses, the red rose of Lancaster enclosing the white rose of York. Half-hidden among the flowers are birds and beasts, deer and a fabulous griffin, part eagle, part lion. It is tempting to speculate that this tapestry, dating from the time of Sir Piers Edgcumbe (1489–1539), who finished the work of his father in building Cotehele, formed part of the furnishings of the new house. The presence of the Tudor rose is certainly appropriate for a family that helped to put the Tudors on the throne, and received honours from both Henry VII and Henry VIII.

Iphigenia
Dutch; around 1650

The tapestry with large figures tells the story of Iphigenia, daughter of Agamemnon, sacrificed by her father at Aulis to obtain a favourable wind for the Greek fleet on its way to the siege of Troy. The goddess Diana, who had caused a calm or contrary wind, took pity on Iphigenia and substituted an animal on the altar, carrying the girl away to Tauros where she became a priestess of Diana. There, her brother Orestes and his friend Pylades were later brought before her as strangers to be sacrificed, and she was able to rescue them and escape. This tapestry shows the dramatic moment of the sacrifice, Diana snatching Iphigenia from the altar and leaving a hind, to the amazement of priest and bystanders. Thought to have been designed by Jan or Solomon de Bray, the series was woven in the Amsterdam workshop of Pieter de Craecht, who delivered a set of Orestes and Iphigenia to the Elector of Brandenburg in 1650.

Verdure with deer and Tudor roses: detail (Queen Anne's Room)

Hunting scene
Flemish; late sixteenth–early seventeenth century

In poor condition, the small figures in the third tapestry are almost indistinguishable. It is a typical design of the late sixteenth or early seventeenth century, with small figures hunting. Two women on foot can be seen on the left, by the window. The border is crudely patched.

KING CHARLES'S ROOM

To either side of the entrance hang pieces of *The Liberal Arts. Grammar* shows the education of children: *Arithmetic*, here duplicated in different borders, is represented by the contemplation of some calculations, assisted by the arithmetician Pythagoras. Below *Arithmetic* hang small fragments of the *Circe* tapestries.

Hero and Leander
Mortlake; 1670s–1680s

Told in antiquity by Musaeus and best known to seventeenth-century England in a long poem by Christopher Marlowe, completed after his death in 1593 by George Chapman, the tragic story of *Hero and Leander* concerns two lovers separated by the

Leander swimming to Hero's tower, watched by her maid: detail from 'The Story of Hero and Leander' (King Charles's Room)

waters of the Hellespont. Francis Cleyn, chief designer at Mortlake, drew the story in six scenes, three of which survive here. Hero, priestess of Venus at Sestos, inspired the love of Leander who set out to swim from Abydos to her tower across the sea. The tapestry on the wall between the two windows shows Leander arriving at the tower, Hero peering coyly round the door while her maid beckons to her to welcome the swimmer. Returned home, Leander tells his parents of his love for Hero, and they plan to charter a ship to abduct her (the piece behind the bed). When Leander swam a second time to the tower, he was drowned, Hero lamenting over his corpse before dying of grief (entrance wall). The tapestries were in this room when Condy drew it, but on different walls.

Cleyn's delicate yet dramatic designs for this series made *Hero and Leander* among the most successful Mortlake tapestries, woven many times. This late version of the 1670s or 1680s, some fifty years after the earliest sets, suffers visually both from a weak border, wrong in scale and emphasis for the figures it surrounds, and from alteration of the designs to comply with commissioned measurements. Tree trunks are added to make the piece with the ship wider, while *Hero mourning Leander* is

cramped by placing Cupid on his rock in the sea above Leander instead of to the side, making this piece smaller. The tapestries have also suffered physically, from overexposure to light rotting the silk and from incompetent 'restoration' which cut away large rectangles of damaged tapestry, filling the holes with canvas. Yet despite all this, Cleyn's consummate designs and the skill of the weavers make these English tapestries rank among the finest in the house.

THE CHAPEL

Adoration of the Magi
Oudenaarde; early seventeenth century

This, the only story from the Bible at Cotehele, was moved recently from Mount Edgcumbe.

Probably dating from the time of Peter Edgcumbe, who died in 1607, or his son, Sir Richard, the tapestry has a stylised landscape found in Flemish tapestries of the late sixteenth and early seventeenth centuries, the foreground filled with decorative leafy plants, the background with individually marked little trees. Most likely part of a *Life of Christ* or *Life of the Virgin*, the tapestry depicts *The Adoration of the Magi*. At the left, the three kings present their gifts, while in the middle distance their attendants and camels still travel towards the ruined stable, seen here at the right, with the heads of ox and ass at the windows behind Joseph, who stands, hat in hand, behind the Virgin and Child. The border, except for the four golden masks at the corners, is similar to one described as 'coarse work of Oudenaarde' in an inventory of Louis XIV: 'in a border of a rod with oak leaves, wound round by a wide golden ribbon or girdle decorated with blue stones and lined with blue'.

CHAPTER SIX

THE TEXTILES

While Cotehele is better known for its tapestries than its furnishing textiles, the house does contain an interesting group of chair and bed upholstery dating mainly from the period 1660–1760.

Among the earliest pieces is the raised-work mirror frame of *c.*1670 in the White Room. Raised work, now commonly called 'stumpwork', was a popular form of amateur needlework in the seventeenth century and is distinguished by having certain areas raised in relief, either by being padded with hair or wool, or by being worked over wooden moulds. The uneven surface thus created limited its use and it is most often to be found on caskets and mirrors or as framed pictures. Biblical scenes and royal 'portraits' were popular subjects, usually surrounded by animals, insects and flowers, all worked with a delightful disregard for scale.

The Cotehele mirror is a typical example of stumpwork. Silvered glass was expensive and the mirror itself is relatively small. The embroidery is worked in coloured silks either directly on to the cream silk ground or on to canvas which has been applied to the ground. Leaves are allowed to flap forward and grass is represented by a cut pile stitch. Four female figures in contemporary dress occupy the centre of each side while the corners are filled by a pear tree, an apple tree, a palace and duck pond. Intervening spaces are taken up by a lion, a griffin and a stag along with birds and flowers. Each of the female figures has an 'attribute' which suggests that they are probably emblematic, a common device at the time. The lady holding a snake for example, may represent Prudence, one of the Virtues, or Earth, one of the Elements, but it is less easy to identify the rest of the quartet. According to an article in *Country Life* in 1924, the mirror is signed and dated: *Margaret Hall 1668*. Since then, the mirror has been placed in a protective case and the signature is obscured.

Another type of needlework popular in the seventeenth century was crewelwork – embroidery in worsted threads, or 'crewels'. Crewelwork was fashionable from around 1660 until the mid-eighteenth century, during which time it underwent several changes in style, which are well represented at Cotehele.

Early designs were worked in monochrome – red, blue or green – and the bed curtains in the South Room are good examples of this type. The all-over design of scrolling stems enclosing alternate lily flowers and lobed trefoils is finely worked in red wool in stem, back and link stitches. The similarity of the design to that of late sixteenth- and

Seventeenth-century mirror, with stumpwork frame (White Room)

early seventeenth-century blackwork, together with the delicacy of execution, indicates that this is an early set, dating from shortly after the middle of the seventeenth century.

The furnishings in the White Room are later and more characteristic of crewelwork. Although bed and window hangings are similar in style, they are from two different sets. Both feature the exotic-tree design derived from patterns on imported Indian painted cottons which, in turn, had been adapted to suit European taste. However, the window curtains (which were probably bed curtains originally) are worked in a restricted palette of blue, green and brown with some yellow, and display a variety of stitches and intricate detail, such as the hounds and deer chasing across the grassy mounds. They date from the first quarter of the eighteenth

(Above) Crewelwork bed hangings in the South Room

(Left) Wool embroidery on the bed in King Charles's Room

century. The bed hangings are more coarsely worked in a wider range of colours and date from c.1730–60. On both sets the embroidery has been cut out and reapplied to modern material.

Although large-scale crewel designs went on being produced well into the eighteenth century, a more refined style had developed using thinner wools, a wide colour range and smaller patterns which were appropriate for use on clothing. This style is represented by the mid-eighteenth-century bedcover in the South Room. The fern-like leaves of earlier crewelwork are retained, but the tree design has been scaled down and the flowers and fruit have become more naturalistic and are joined by chinoiserie birds.

A third bed at Cotehele, that in the King Charles Room, also displays wool embroidery of the late seventeenth–early eighteenth centuries, but in a different technique. The borders are worked on canvas in a coarse cross stitch with silk highlights. They have been reapplied to a later background material. The design of scrolling branches and turned-back leaves bears similarities to the later crewelwork designs, but is more stylised because of the need to square-up the pattern for cross-stitch. The fringing on the valances is probably contemporary with the needlework; plain silk hangers, striped to match the needlework, hang from an ornate trellis-pattern heading.

Trimmings played an important role in upholstery of the late seventeenth century. A superb example, dating from c.1670, embellishes the bed in the Red Room. The fringe itself is insignificant alongside the magnificent braid which trims the valances. It is constructed of silk-wrapped wire and vellum strips formed into flower and leaf motifs. At the corners, silk-wrapped and netted wooden 'olives' act as ornamental buttons; originally loops on the adjoining valance would have hooked over them. In place of the plumes which usually surmount the canopy of a grand bed, the Cotehele bed has four 'cups' supporting cascades of bows, rosettes and tufts on a wire framework. Elaborate trimmings were a hallmark of French upholstery, but whether these examples were imported or made by, or under the influence of, French craftsmen working in England is not certain. The bed hang-

One of the ornamental 'cup' finials, supporting cascades of bows, rosettes and tufts, that decorate the corners of the bed in the Red Room

ings are of a wool material. This is unusual since such elaborate trimmings are normally associated with rich silk fabrics. Wool was sometimes used for expensive furnishings but in this instance the trimmings have been reused at a later date.

The most important set of seat upholstery at Cotehele is the suite in the Punch Room. The furniture itself is of three different dates but the covering of knotted wool dates from c.1750–60 (with the exception of one chair cover worked earlier this century). Knotting was a popular pastime during the first half of the eighteenth cen-

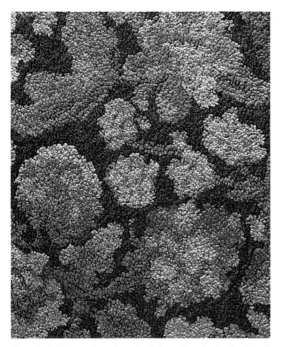

Detail of 'Queen Anne's tatting' from the suite in the Punch Room

tury. It was a forerunner of tatting and the suite is known locally as 'Queen Anne's tatting', although there is no proven link with Queen Anne. Wool, silk or linen thread was knotted at close intervals with the aid of a larger version of a tatting shuttle. This was a simple, repetitive task that required little concentration and could be performed while travelling or making polite conversation. The knotted threads were then either couched down individually or stitched to each other and then applied to fabric. As a rule, the knotting covers only a small area of the fabric, but at Cotehele the knotting completely conceals the backing. The floral pattern relates closely to designs for conventional canvas-work of the mid-eighteenth century, while the flower vases on the screen panels can be traced back to late seventeenth-century Dutch flower painting.

Cotehele has had no tradition of continuous occupation since the seventeenth century and the question therefore arises of when and why the textiles were introduced. The South Room, Red Room and King Charles Room beds are all clearly ident-

ifiable in the Condy lithographs, the stumpwork mirror and Punch Room chairs probably so, thus proving that all these items were at Cotehele by 1840. (The White Room bed is shown, but the hangings are not depicted in any detail.)

It is unlikely that the furnishings would have been bought new for a largely unoccupied house but some may have been brought from Mount Edgcumbe when they fell from fashion. However, the sheer quantity of textiles suggests a more deliberate introduction. Certain fabrics, for example the worsted chair covers in the Red Room, hint at activity towards the middle of the eighteenth century. This would certainly fit in with the known antiquarian interests of the 3rd Baron Edgcumbe who may have brought in, or even bought old needlework and trimmings to add an aura of antiquity to the house.

As a result of their infrequent use and the absence of electric light, the textiles at Cotehele have survived in unusually good condition. The embroideries inevitably take pride of place alongside the tapestries, but the house also contains examples of silk and worsted fabrics, leather and horsehair. Together they form a significant collection of historical furnishings which deserves to be better known.

CHAPTER SEVEN
THE ARMS AND ARMOUR

In the troubled world of late medieval Cornwall, leading families like the Edgcumbes could hope to maintain their authority only by armed force. Cotehele was built with defence in mind and the Hall served not only as a communal eating place, but also as an armoury, hung with weapons for the use of the fighting household and the wider circle of retainers on which the lord of the house could call. The visible display of such weapons in as prominent a position as the Hall at Cotehele was a potent reminder of the Edgcumbes' power.

Whether any of the armour hanging in the Hall today actually belonged to Sir Richard or Sir Piers Edgcumbe is uncertain. It seems possible that most of it was assembled in the eighteenth century. Nevertheless the collection remains among the most impressive and diverse in the West Country.

When Sir Richard Edgcumbe was fighting at Bosworth, no doubt in full plate armour that covered him from head to foot, he was well protected from sword cuts. However, he would have been vulnerable to the pole-axe, with its strong chopping blade and sharp spike mounted at the end of a stout haft, which could pierce the strongest armour. (An example is on the right by the entrance to the Hall.) A similar weapon, the glaive, can be seen near the Zulu shield, and close by is an English bill (a type of long-handled axe). This last weapon was very popular with English foot soldiers.

Another weapon that the knight learnt to fear was the gun, which had first appeared in England early in the fourteenth century. By the sixteenth century guns were commonly used by most armies and their bullets were capable of penetrating all but the stoutest armour of the time. The earliest firearms at Cotehele are the two matchlock guns dating from the late sixteenth and early seventeenth centuries, their wooden stocks and butts inlaid with mother-of-pearl and chiselled steel.

During the Civil War, soldiers wearing full armour were rarely seen on the battlefield. Most troops wore a thick breastplate, strong enough to stop a bullet from a musket, and a thinner backplate which was not bullet-proof, as soldiers were not expected to turn their backs to the enemy. The cavalry trooper wore a lobster-tail helmet with a sweeping neck guard, cheek pieces and a peak to which was fitted a three-bar guard to protect the face against a sword cut. There are several sets of such armour around the walls of the Hall. In addition to the body armour many cavalrymen wore on their left arm a gauntlet with a long cuff. It was important to protect this arm, for it held the reins and so could not easily be moved to avoid a sword cut. One of these elbow or bridle gauntlets is hanging by the window on the west wall. Most of the cavalrymen were armed with a sword and a pair of wheel-lock pistols similar to those on the north wall by the entrance to the Kitchen.

When a knight was buried, his tomb was often marked with a stone or wooden statue, and later it became the custom to hang part of his armour above the tomb. By the seventeenth century this practice was dying out, but many country families kept up the tradition. To reduce the cost, old helmets were adapted to hang above the tombs. The four Civil War helmets at the west end of the Hall have all been altered for this purpose. The local blacksmith fixed a spike on to the skull and on to this went the carved crest of the family.

Beneath this group of helmets and armour hangs a sword of the late sixteenth century which is so large that it could only be wielded with both hands. These two-handed swords were popular with the Swiss and German troops of the period.

By the eighteenth century firearms dominated the battlefield, but officers, non-commissioned officers and many local officials still carried weapons which were primarily ceremonial and not intended for use. Around the walls are several examples of halberds – axe-like weapons on long shafts, which were carried by Sergeants of the British Army and civic dignitaries.

Several members of the Edgcumbe family were widely travelled and they may have brought back a number of weapons in the Hall. Above the fireplace are matchlock guns from India and Java. At the side are daggers from south-east Asia known as *kris*. These were sometimes made with a wavy serpent-like blade; others were fitted with a straight stabbing blade, but all have the strange angled hilt. Souvenirs of Grand Tour visits to Europe may include the Spanish guns, as well as the rare sixteenth-century Italian shield. In the nineteenth century the Edgcumbes travelled in the Far East and these visits probably produced such weapons as the *kora* on the north wall, an executioner's sword from Nepal. It has a hooked blade and is related to the Gurkha *kukri*. There are also numerous good-

quality weapons from India, Persia and North Africa. On the south wall are two crossed swords from India known as *firanghis*. These swords were designed so that they could be used with one hand, but if a really hard blow was required, then a spike at the top of the hilt could be grasped by the other hand to deliver a much more powerful cut.

On the west wall are two daggers called *katars*, which are held with the blade sticking forward from the knuckles and are used with a punching movement. The one on the left, with a curved decorative plate to guard the hand, comes from southern India. Also from India are the long *patas* or gauntlet swords. These rather strange weapons were the favourites of the Maharattas, a warrior race. The *pata* has a gauntlet-like hilt into which the hand is slipped to grip a crossbar so that the blade sticks straight forward like an extension of the forearm.

At the far end of the Hall on the east wall are two large colours or flags of the 4th (Royal South

A selection of the armour at Cotehele, c.1880

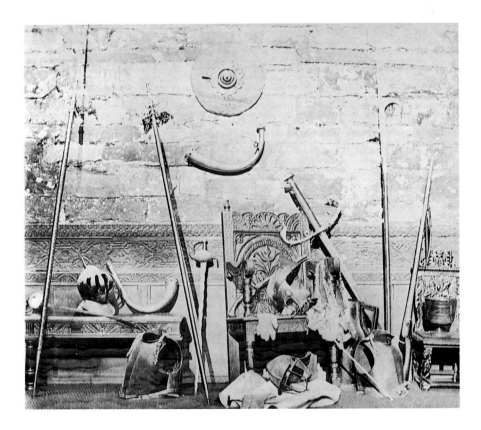

The Hall hung with armour in the late nineteenth century

Middlesex) Militia, which date from the time of the Napoleonic Wars. This unit, which was commanded by a member of the Edgcumbe family, was one of the numerous militia and volunteer troops assembled to oppose the threatened invasion by the French. Such troops would have been armed with a flintlock musket known as the 'Brown Bess'. There are two early examples of these British Army muskets, together with their socket bayonets, hanging above the wheel-lock pistols and crossbow.

The 5th Earl of Mount Edgcumbe fought in South Africa: the *assegai* (spear) and an oxhide shield in the south-east corner of the Hall are a reminder of the Zulu war of 1879. From North Africa is the Arab musket known as a *kabyle*, which is finely decorated with brass and silver. Nearby is the star-shaped leather and brass decorated flask, in which the owner carried his gunpowder. From the Sudan comes what resembles a crusader's sword with a simple cross hilt. It hangs facing the elbow gauntlet.

By the entrance to the Hall there is a cavalry sword which recalls a more recent conflict. It bears a plaque commemorating the death of Lieutenant Piers Edgcumbe in the fighting around Dunkirk during the Second World War.

CHAPTER EIGHT

THE HOUSE

The Exterior

THE SOUTH WING

The gate opens to the straight, short drive with the buttressed range of the barn built by Sir Richard Edgcumbe (1485–9) on its right. Ahead stands his embattled gatehouse in the middle of the south wing of the house. Sir Richard's work is distinguished from the late thirteenth- or early fourteenth-century fabric (of rough rubble and small round-headed lancets) by the even courses of cut granite blocks and the pointed arch of the entrance with its projecting, moulded dripcourse and heavy label stops. The tympanum and spandrels of this doorway are deeply cut into conventional Gothic patterns.

THE RETAINERS' COURT

To the left of the south wing lie the outbuildings of the Retainers' Court, which comprises the western part of the house. Into this court projects Sir Richard Edgcumbe's Chapel with its charming little bellcote and gay finials, all in moulded granite. Here there is further evidence of late fifteenth-century work in the two-light, pointed windows under square dripcourses with label stops, and in the low broad west window to the Chapel. The wide pointed arch to the Hall Court, with a porter's squint beside it, was probably the original entrance of Hilaria de Cotehele's day, approached from the north by the road from Trehill which still exists under the surface of the fields which abut the house.

At the north end of the Retainers' Court a pointed archway leads to The Meadow, with a good view of the north-west tower added to the house in the 1620s, perhaps by Sir Thomas Coteel.

THE HALL COURT

Under the square gate-tower, a wicket door leads into the Hall Court through a narrow passage with ponderous moulded vaulting and on its right side two doorways. The passageway is cobbled and just wide enough to allow a laden pack-horse to walk through it. From the court numerous flattened archways lead to various quarters of the house, but the visitor is only concerned with the doorway immediately ahead that gives into the Hall.

A curious feature of this beautiful little court is the abrupt juxtaposition of the walls in the north-west corner which marks the halting of Sir Richard Edgcumbe's work and the beginning of that of his son, Sir Piers. On the west wall is the perpendicular east window under a pointed gable of Sir Richard's Chapel. The north wall marks the boundary of Sir Piers's additions. Below its gable are six-light windows, each in two stages, on both floors, lighting Sir Piers's Parlour and the Solar above it. To the right a similar window on the ground floor, but of four lights, marks the dais end of the Hall, which is otherwise lit by three two-light windows at a higher level under the eaves. All these windows are complete with saddle bars, have heads of ogival shape, and the low transoms and concave moulded mullions that proclaim their early Tudor origin.

On the west side of the court the archway leads through to the Retainers' Court. To its left is the door into the laundry which was originally the porter's lodge of the old house, before Sir Richard Edgcumbe built his new entrance tower in the south wing in the 1480s. To the right are the priest's lodgings.

On the opposite side of the court is the east wing, the interior of which was extensively rebuilt for the 3rd Earl's widow in 1862.

(*Above*) *The north range of the Hall Court, with the Great Parlour crosswing (under gable on the left) and Hall (on the right)*

The Interior

THE HALL

Unusually, the Hall is entered directly from the Court rather than through a screens passage dividing it from the service rooms on the right. Although Sir Piers Edgcumbe's late fifteenth-century Hall is comparatively small and has lost the raised dais at the western end, it is one of the most splendid interiors of the West Country and intensely evocative of the late Middle Ages, when the walls would have been hung with arms and armour ready to use in times of alarm and not merely as decoration. The floor is a rough uneven composition of lime ash, which is soft and needs constant repair. The walls are plain and lime washed. Over the fireplace is the seventeenth-century coat of arms of the Edgcumbe

The Hall

THE TOWER

THE PUNCH ROOM

THE KITCHEN COURT

THE KITCHEN

THE OLD DINING ROOM

THE HALL

THE LOBBY

THE CHAPEL

THE RETAINERS' COURT

THE HALL COURT

THE EAST RANGE

now used as THE FILM ROOM

N

Ground Floor

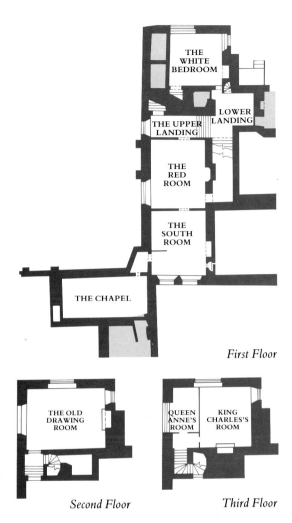

First Floor

Second Floor   *Third Floor*

family in carved wood, which is probably funerary in origin.

ROOF

The roof is old-fashioned for the period; instead of the developed hammerbeam type, composed of massive truncated beams, it is carried on a network of smaller timbers, whose purlins are strengthened with moulded wind-braces, the total effect being light and decorative.

STAINED GLASS

The late fifteenth-century heraldic panes of the windows are emblazoned with the arms of the families into which the Edgcumbes married, names that evoke the past history and glories of the West

Country – Holland, Tremayne, Durnford, Cotterell, Ralegh, Trevanion, Carew, St Maur, Courtenay and Fitzwalter – each contained within a diamond-shaped shield, a fleur-de-lis on the upper corner.

ARMS AND ARMOUR

It is not clear exactly when the collection was assembled here. The earliest pieces date from the late fifteenth century, but most are mid-seventeenth-century or later, and of very mixed origin. Some pieces no doubt arrived here during the Civil War when Col. Piers Edgcumbe commanded a regiment for Charles I at Plymouth; others may have been collected by the 1st and 3rd Barons Edgcumbe in the eighteenth century. Most of the weapons seen today in the Hall can be clearly identified in J. C. Buckler's view of 1821.

NORTH (FACING) WALL

Above the chair-table is a vambrace or fore-arm defence, for use by a man who had lost his left hand. The fingers and thumbs can be locked into place to provide a firm grip on reins or sword. It was probably made in Germany in the seventeenth century.

There are also a pair of wheel-lock holster pistols, *c*.1650, a pair of eighteenth-century 'Brown Bess' flintlock muskets, English and Spanish rapiers of the seventeenth and eighteenth centuries, two crossbows, halberds, partisans and a variety of swords and firearms.

EAST (RIGHT-HAND) WALL

The two large colours belong to the 4th (Royal South Middlesex) Militia, which was commanded by a member of the Edgcumbe family during the Napoleonic Wars.

SOUTH (ENTRANCE) WALL

The three breastplates, *c*.1640, are each mounted below contemporary lobster-tail helmets. The various weapons include an Elizabethan pole-arm, two tulwars or Indian sabres, a pair of Indian fore-arm swords, *c*.1800, an early pole-arm, possibly fifteenth-century, and a Zulu skin shield, with accompanying spear. To the left of these is a North African powder flask.

WEST (LEFT HAND) WALL

Above the oak court cupboard is a figure wearing English half-armour, *c*.1600. The Civil War helmets are funerary pieces, adapted to hang above tombs.

FURNITURE AND PEWTER

The furniture is mainly oak of the seventeenth century, with little concession to comfort, but some of it elaborately carved. The most notable piece is the armchair against the south wall, which may date from the late sixteenth century and is carved with early Renaissance motifs, such as the medallion head of the gentleman in the back panel. The pewter plates and mugs on the central refectory table are mainly mid-eighteenth-century, and the former bear the coat of arms of the Edgcumbe family.

The door beyond the fireplace leads to the foot of the main staircase over a cobbled floor uncovered in 1956. Turn left into the Old Dining Room.

THE OLD DINING ROOM

The room was no doubt the principal Parlour when it was added by Sir Piers Edgcumbe in the early sixteenth century; communal eating in the Hall was already in decline by this date. It seems to have assumed its current shape following the remodelling of the west range in 1650–1. It is referred to as a Parlour in the ground plan of Cotehele which accompanied Arundell's account of the house. The room acquired its present name after the rebuilding of the east wing in 1862. By about 1880 it had become a sort of writing room or study, with two of the curious folding tables, thought to have been made on the estate in the early eighteenth century, brought into the centre of the room for the purpose. As antiquarian interest in the house and its contents grew in the latter half of the nineteenth century, constant small changes were made in the arrangement and use of the rooms, no doubt stimulated by the fact that the dowager Countess had retreated to the remodelled east wing for the convenience of daily living.

The buffet or cup-board (now in the Punch Room) in the foreground of Condy's view of this room, was the usual means of displaying and storing plate and other vessels until it was supplanted by the sideboard in the eighteenth century. Unfortunately most of these brass, pewter and earthenware vessels are no longer at Cotehele, but the Condy view shows them arranged not only on the buffet but on window ledges and on the eighteenth-century folding tables. They fascinated nineteenth-

The Old Dining Room

'Antiquities' arranged around one of Cotehele's carved buffets, c.1880

century antiquaries, and an extract from a contemporary study is quoted in Arundell's account: 'Of drinking cups, diverse and sundry sorts we have; some of elmes, some of box, some of maple, some of holly etc. Mazers, broad mouthed dishes, noggins, whiskins, piggins, quinzes, ale-bowles, wassail-bowles, quart dishes, tankards, cannes . . .' One of the 'wassail-bowles' is still in the Punch Room.

TAPESTRIES

The first of many panels of tapestry at Cotehele is encountered in this room. Here, and in subsequent rooms, they cover almost every inch of wall, and over the years have been treated more as practical wall coverings than as works of art. Hence they have been ruthlessly cut and rejoined or looped over doors and overlapped to suit the space which they had to fill. Most of the sets are no longer complete, if indeed they ever were, and many are split between several rooms. (For a fuller history and description of the tapestries, see Chapter Five.)

RIGHT OF ENTRANCE DOOR

Orpheus and Eurydice
Antwerp, *c.*1700

OVER FIREPLACE

The Story of Circe
Antwerp, probably 1680s
This tapestry has been cut down to form the equivalent of a Georgian overmantel picture or plaster relief, pointing to an eighteenth-century arrangement.

OTHER WALLS

Pastoral scenes with Diana and Apollo
Antwerp, last quarter seventeenth century

UNDER WEST WINDOW

Fragment of border
Evidently commissioned by the Edgcumbe family since it bears the family's boar's head crest.

FLOOR

The old boarded floor being rotten, it was replaced in cement after the Second World War, and the present elm boarding was laid in 1977. The carpet, which is not indigenous to the house, is a Donegal.

FURNITURE

The furniture is a mixture of seventeenth- and eighteenth-century pieces, and includes a rare William and Mary high-back settee upholstered in silk velvet with needlework panels. By the fireplace is a seventeenth-century French dwarf chair of walnut, heavily carved with a scene from the story of Susannah and the Elders. The painted mirror in a walnut frame, c.1700, on the west wall is probably English.

CLOCK

The bracket clock is a one-handed lantern clock, dated 1668, by George Harris of Fritwell, Oxfordshire. The crude pine case is of a later date.

CERAMICS

On the central table are two rare tin-glazed earthenware dishes from the Lambeth factory painted in majolica colours and dated respectively 1670 and 1673. The blue and white dishes on the small tables are Delft, of the kind described by Queen Charlotte on her visit to Cotehele in 1789. The soup tureen is 'Bristol Delft'.

The door left of the entrance leads to the Punch Room.

THE PUNCH ROOM

The room takes its present name from the panels of tapestries depicting scenes of Bacchic revelry concerned with the making of wine, and its purpose is further endorsed by the presence of the eighteenth-century brick wine bins in a closet in the far left-hand corner. The room was known as the Little Parlour in Condy's plan, suggesting its original function as a room of some intimacy. However, it was entitled the Ante-Room in the accompanying lithograph and arranged formally with furniture against the walls. It may perhaps have acted for a period as a reception room serving the bedroom beyond, as was common practice in houses of the late seventeenth and eighteenth century. Like the

The Punch Room

Old Dining Room and the rooms above in the west range it seems to have been remodelled in 1650–1. John Cornforth has suggested that the cornice and the fireplace may date from the eighteenth-century re-creation of the ancient interiors.

CARPET

This is a Persian 'Mahal' carpet, not indigenous to the house.

TAPESTRIES

The tapestries depicted by Condy are mostly from the *Liberal Arts* series now hung in different rooms, so the present panels cannot have been hung here before 1840.

The Bacchanals
English, 1670s–'80s
The Bacchanals were the infant servants of Bacchus, the god of wine.

OVER DOOR TO STAIRS

A section of tapestry border, with an early Edgcumbe crest at the centre. The effect is very similar to an eighteenth-century plaster or carved wood frieze.

FURNITURE

The furniture in 1840 was a mixture of ages and styles, some heavy oak pieces, an East Indies 'Burgomaster' chair (since removed to the Old Drawing Room), the needlework and velvet settee (now in the Old Dining Room), and one from the set of mid-eighteenth-century chairs with their distinctive knotted wool upholstery, which now comprises the principal furnishing of the room. The upholstery, which was also applied to the settee and the two pole screens in the room, is known locally as 'Queen Anne's tatting'.

The rest of the furniture is seventeenth-century. The two-tier oak buffet was made in England in the early seventeenth century and was in the Old Dining Room until at least 1840.

VESSELS

Most of the vessels shown in the Condy view are no longer in the house, though there are some interesting survivals including two copper ale-warmers, a lignum-vitae wassail bowl and some ornate nineteenth-century Delft vases.

The granite stairs lead to the White Room.

THE WHITE ROOM

The White Room forms the ground floor of the Tower added to the house in the 1620s and is named after the curtains and bed hangings.

CEILING

The White Room is the only one in the house to have a decorative ceiling. It is formed of moulded wooden ribs in a geometrical pattern, pinned to the ceiling and serving no structural function. Previously considered to be seventeenth-century, the ceiling decoration may be an example of mid-eighteenth-century antiquarianism.

TAPESTRIES

ON RIGHT-HAND WALL

The Bacchanals
English, 1670s–'80s
Part of the series in the Punch Room.

ON LEFT-HAND WALL

Pygmalion
Antwerp or London, 1670s–'90s

OVER GRANITE STAIRS AND FIREPLACE

Fragments from *Venus and Phaon*
Antwerp or London, 1670s–'90s

BESIDE FIREPLACE

Fragment from *Liberal Arts* series
Antwerp, 1660s–'70s

BEHIND BED

Caesar Augustus
Antwerp, 1660s–'70s

BED

The walnut bed is probably Goanese and may have been acquired through the flourishing Portuguese trade with Plymouth. The bed-hangings, like the window curtains, are of eighteenth-century crewel-work embroidered on to a linen backing. The bedspread is of fine eighteenth-century Durham quilting.

FURNITURE

The set of ebonised high-back chairs, *c.*1690, has lost the embroidered seats shown in the Condy view of the room. The beautifully figured early eighteenth-century walnut secretaire to the left of the principal window is still in the same position

The White Room

as it was in 1840. The mirror on the wall opposite the bed has an unusual surround of embroidered stumpwork and is signed and dated 'Margaret Hall 1668', but this is now obscured.

The door right of the fireplace leads to the Lower Landing.

THE LOWER LANDING

FURNITURE

Outside the White Room is a late sixteenth-century French oak cabinet, richly carved with architectural motifs, biblical and mythological figures. It is possibly the earliest piece of furniture in the house. There are also here three Welsh chairs of elaborately turned ash with triangular seats. From the late eighteenth century they were avidly collected for their curiosity value, especially by members of Horace Walpole's circle, as they were often supposed to be of monastic origin. Certainly the type existed by the mid-Tudor period, if not earlier.

Turn right up the staircase; left is the Red Room.

THE RED ROOM

The Red Room and that adjoining it were originally one, with a roof supported by three ties of arched braces similar to those in the Hall; it was quite common to find great chambers on the first floor open to the roof in West Country manor houses. Served by a single west-facing window, the room is naturally gloomy, but this only serves to enhance its rather mysterious atmosphere. It is interesting to note the cracked and dirty plaster ceilings and the broad rough pine floorboards which are invariably seen in Condy's illustrations and which survive in this and the adjacent room.

TAPESTRIES

LEFT OF FIREPLACE, AND EITHER SIDE OF SOUTH ROOM DOOR

Children's Games
Antwerp, 1660s–'70s

BEHIND ENTRANCE DOOR

The Death of Remus from *Romulus and Remus* series
Brussels, 1660s

The Red Room,
c.1840, lithograph
by Nicholas Condy

BED

The Red Room is dominated by the large bed which gives it its name. The bed curtains and valances, dating from *c.*1670, are of napped wool. The valances are decorated with intricate 'passementerie' – pieces of vellum, or parchment, and wire ornamented with silk and metal thread. The elaborate cup-shaped finials have wire branches with applied rosettes. The arrangement and atmosphere of the room may have been a deliberate eighteenth-century creation.

FURNITURE

The furniture is the same mixture of late seventeenth- and eighteenth-century pieces, and includes an unusual escritoire of about 1660 inlaid with sprays of flowers and probably of Spanish origin. It is mounted on a plain gate-leg stand, possibly also Spanish. The tall black-painted chairs on scrolled legs, of about 1680, one type with carved backsplats and the other with an upholstered back. The chair covers are watered worsted. They can be seen in Condy's view of the room, together with the sofa of about 1720. Again, the Red Room is very much as Condy showed it about 150 years ago.

Beyond the Red Room is the South Room.

THE SOUTH ROOM

The principal private room or 'Solar' of Sir Piers Edgcumbe's house, it was known as the Best Bedroom before the Victorian replanning of the interior. With its large multi-paned south-facing window it makes a surprising contrast to the gloominess of the preceding room. Its importance in the medieval house is emphasised by the small recesses which contain peep holes down into the Hall and the Chapel, so that public ceremony could be observed by the lord in privacy.

TAPESTRIES

FROM LEFT OF ENTRANCE DOOR

The Rape of the Sabines, Romulus and Remus dividing the robbers' spoils and *Building of Rome* from the *Romulus and Remus* series
Brussels, 1660s

OVER FIREPLACE

Augustus sacrifices to the 'Unknown God' from *Caesar Augustus* series
Antwerp, 1660s–'70s

BETWEEN BED AND ENTRANCE DOOR

Numa Pompilius
Antwerp, 1660s–'70s

The South Room

BED

The plain bedstead with front posts of sycamore wood is hung with a beautiful cloth of white linen embroidered in red wool in a delicate flowing design, dating from shortly after the mid-seventeenth century. The original ground fabric has mostly worn away and the design has been skilfully attached to the lining with a fine running stitch. The mid-eighteenth-century bedspread is of light crewelwork on a twill union.

TEXTILES

The Condy view of the room shows a set of matching covers for chairs and stools of different dates. These can probably be identified with the Genoese cut velvet which survives on a set of six mid-seventeenth-century chairs in the room today. Rather curiously, Condy shows one of the rare fifteenth-century altar frontals, presumably original to the Chapel at Cotehele, draped over the bed in this room (not on view to the public).

Return through the Red Room to the Upper Landing.

THE UPPER LANDING

TESTER

The oak ceiling board, or tester, from a four-poster bed, still in existence in Dyfed (but perhaps previously a cupboard front), is inscribed in Welsh, which translates as: 'The expert who made it (:) Harry ap Griffith'. The board is interesting, both for its heraldic content and its biblical symbolism. Two of the eight panels into which it is divided were probably later additions or substitutions, one being the central top panel representing the Tudor Royal Arms with the French fleur-de-lis in the second and fourth quarters which was not formalised until 1707, the other being the central bottom panel which represents *The Expulsion of Adam and Eve from the Garden of Eden*. The corner panels depict, at top left, *The Instruments of the Passion*; at top right, *Musicians playing Welsh instruments*, representing Harmony; at bottom left, *St George and the Dragon*; at bottom right, *An unexplained scene with a woman, a lamb, and a dragon standing before a fortress with a group of kings and courtiers*. The frame of the tester, carved in shallower relief, depicts scenes of hawking and hunting.

TAPESTRY

Geometry from the *Liberal Arts* series
Antwerp, 1660s–'70s

CERAMICS

The blue and white English delftware tray painted with a group of Roman deities, is copied from a

Detail of the Welsh tester board

The Old Drawing Room

celebrated silver bas-relief known as the Corbridge Lanx, which was discovered in 1735 in the River Tyne, near Newcastle, on land belonging to the Duke of Somerset, whose arms consequently appear on the rim of the tray.

At the end of the Upper Landing on the right, a massive granite arch leads on to the Tower Stairs, and the second floor of the early seventeenth-century addition reputedly built by a Flemish merchant, Sir Thomas Coteel, whose daughter married Sir Richard Edgcumbe (1570–1638).

THE OLD DRAWING ROOM

The stout oak door, which leads into the entrance lobby of the room, features Tudor roses set in diamond-shaped panels. The screen which protrudes into the Old Drawing Room comprises panels of linenfold carving that predate the Tower

(built in the 1620s). They were probably assembled and installed at a later date.

The Drawing Room retained its name after the Victorian replanning, but it was designated 'Old' to distinguish it from the New Drawing Room in the remodelled east wing, and its function seems to have shrunk to that of a private bed/sitting room. Most of the same old furniture is in the room, and the concession to Victorian taste is seen in its looser arrangement rather than in the introduction of new pieces.

TAPESTRIES

OVER FIREPLACE:

Romulus and Remus before Numitor from *Romulus and Remus* series
Brussels, 1660s

67

From *The Story of Mankind* series
Brussels, 1630s:

LEFT OF INNER LOBBY, BEHIND PORCH
Triumph of Virtue

ON OPPOSITE WALL, IN LEFT-HAND CORNER
Temperance and the Gods

ON SAME WALL, IN RIGHT-HAND CORNER
Time driving away the Pleasures from Age

RIGHT OF FIREPLACE
Ceres, Bacchus and Venus

FURNITURE

George III and Queen Charlotte were entertained to breakfast here during a visit in August 1789, and two cushions of maroon velvet were inscribed, unusually in ink, to commemorate the event. The ebony settee on which it is believed the Royal couple sat is part of a large set of furniture in this room whose provenance is difficult to establish; it was of a type whose mysterious origin and exotic appearance excited antiquarian interest as early as the later eighteenth century. Even into this century such furniture was thought to be of Tudor origin, although the earliest examples are now considered to date from the first quarter of the seventeenth century, possibly made in Ceylon or Batavia (now Djakarta) in Indonesia, following Dutch or Portuguese prototypes.

Other furniture includes, against the long wall, a Dutch walnut cabinet made about 1710. Inlaid with ebony and ivory stringing and fitted with an architectural interior recess on a later English stand, it is the most elaborate of the several cabinets and writing desks of this period in the house. An Italian cabinet with an architectural interior, but of altogether different style and date, is in the corner of the opposite wall. Dating to about 1600, it is veneered with walnut, ebonised to give it a particularly rich appearance, and carved in very high relief with human figures at the angles and bearded masks at the feet. The piece figures prominently in Condy's view of the room, as does the set of ebony seat furniture. The room also contains a Nonsuch chest and a Burgomaster chair.

Continue up the staircase to Queen Anne's Room.

QUEEN ANNE'S ROOM

BED

Decorated with early Tudor carved, gilt and painted posts, but with seventeenth-century finials and headboard, it is now only partially hung, the curtain material being an early eighteenth-century woollen damask, and the much damaged valances of late seventeenth-century yellow silk. The fine patchwork quilt is Victorian.

TAPESTRIES

RIGHT OF BED
Sacrifice of Iphigenia
Dutch, c.1650

LEFT OF BED
Hunting scene
Flemish, late sixteenth–early seventeenth century

Queen Anne's Room

King Charles's Room

KING CHARLES'S ROOM

The room takes its name from the belief that Charles I slept here in September 1644 on his march from Liskeard to Exeter. It is perhaps the room in the house most evocative of genuine antiquity, and there is little reason to suppose that its essential furnishing has altered since its creation in the early seventeenth century, although the bed has moved several times.

TAPESTRIES

From *Hero and Leander* series
Mortlake, 1670s–'80s

BEHIND BED HEAD
Leander taking leave of his parents

BETWEEN WINDOWS
Leander swimming the Hellespont

LEFT OF BED
Hero mourning Leander's death

OVER FIREPLACE AND AROUND DOOR
Grammar and Arithmetic from *Liberal Arts* series
Antwerp, 1660s–'70s

BED

It is a complicated construction, made up apparently of bulbous Elizabethan posts from a table and a seventeenth-century headboard that may originally have been an overmantel for a fireplace. The late seventeenth or early eighteenth-century hangings are of crewelwork with some silk in cross-stitch and *petit point*. The woollen backing is relatively modern.

MIRROR

The mirror on the chest by the far window, dating from about 1625, has a polished metal plate, since looking glass was extremely rare before the mid-seventeenth century.

Descend the staircases to the Lower Landing.

THE MAIN STAIRCASE

The stairs are lit by three windows overlooking the Kitchen Court in the centre of the house.

PICTURES

TO LEFT OF RED ROOM DOOR

FRISIAN, *c.*1590
Sir Thomas Coteel
Panel
The sitter, who is identified both in the *cartellino* and on a letter on the table addressed to him in London, was the father of Mary, the second wife of Sir Richard Edgcumbe (*c.*1570–1638). He was a merchant from Brabant who fled from the Spanish Inquisition towards the end of Elizabeth's reign – presumably shortly after this portrait was painted, unless the artist also came over to England. He is said to have lived for a long time at Cotehele (the homophony is pure coincidence).

ON STAIRS, LEFT-HAND SIDE

The tomb of Sir Richard Edgcumbe at Morlaix
Watercolour on vellum
Sir Richard Edgcumbe died fighting for Anne of Brittany in 1489 and was buried at Morlaix. His tomb was destroyed in the French Revolution, but had previously been copied in this watercolour, which seems to have provided the source for the panel painting in the Chapel.

ENGLISH, *c.*1670
Mary Glanville, Mrs Piers Edgcumbe
Oval
Daughter of Sir John Glanville (1586–1661) of Tavistock, King's Sergeant and Speaker of the Short Parliament. She was married to Col. Piers

Edgcumbe, MP, but widowed in 1667. They left a son, Sir Richard Edgcumbe, father of the 1st Baron, and a daughter, Winifred, wife of Thomas, 5th Baron (and subsequently 1st Earl of) Coventry.

ON STAIRS, RIGHT-HAND SIDE:

ENGLISH, ? eighteenth century
Reputed portrait of Margaret Edgcumbe,
Lady Denny (1560–1648)
Panel
The daughter of Sir Piers, or Peter, Edgcumbe, MP (by 1536–1607/8) and Margaret Luttrell of Dunster, and married to Sir Edward Denny (d.1599), younger son of Henry VIII's favourite, Sir Anthony Denny, who was rewarded with the lion's share of the forfeited Irish estates of the 15th Earl of Desmond (d.1583). She was Maid of Honour to Queen Elizabeth I, to whom her husband was Gentleman of the Bedchamber. This portrait appears to be a later pastiche.

ENGLISH, 1608
Portrait of an Unknown Man (? Sir Richard Edgcumbe)
Panel
Inscribed: *Aet. suae 33 An Dieu 1606*, and with four lines of French verse.
Although this has variously been called a portrait of Sir Anthony (1500–49) or Sir Edward (d.1599) Denny, it can clearly be of neither. Nor could it be of Sir Edward's sons, Sir Arthur or Anthony, since the former, the eldest, was only born in 1584. Provided that the picture was an heirloom, and not simply bought to lend an air of antiquity to the house, it seems reasonable to suggest that it might just represent Sir Richard Edgcumbe (*c.*1570–1638) the brother of Margaret, Lady Denny. His first wife was Anne Cary of Cockington, and his second Mary, daughter of the shadowy Flemish merchant in London, Sir Thomas Coteel or Cottle.

OVER OLD DINING ROOM DOOR

After SIR PETER LELY (1618–80)
Sir Richard Edgcumbe, KB (1640–88)
Oval
Dubbed a Knight of the Bath (whose sash he wears) before the coronation of Charles II, no doubt in recognition that his father, Col. Piers Edgcumbe, MP, had been 'a lover of the King and Church, which he endeavoured to support, in the time of the Civil Wars, to the utmost of his power and fortune' (in the words of his monument). He was married to

the Lady Anne Montagu, second surviving daughter of the 1st Earl of Sandwich; their only surviving son became the 1st Baron Edgcumbe. Lely's original is at Mount Edgcumbe.

At the foot of the Main Staircase, in the cobbled Lobby, turn left into the Kitchen Court.

THE KITCHEN COURT

Leading off the foot of the stairs, this is the smallest of Cotehele's three courts and lies in the centre of the house. To the east and south are the Kitchen and Hall chimneys; to the north west the top of Sir Thomas Coteel's tower rises above the roofs.

The fine lead tank, bearing the initials 'TC' and the date 1639, may be connected with Sir Thomas Coteel, whose will is dated 19 June 1639.

The tapered hexagonal stones, with hollowed-out interiors, are possibly rare local types of cressets, early medieval lamps formed by a lighted wick floating in a pool of oil in a container. Whatever their function, one of these stones has a clear connection with Cotehele. Around its 'waist' there is inscribed ALEXANDER CHAMPNON ME FIER [I] FECIT. Alexander Champernowne (1382–1441) owned the manor of Bere Ferrers, on the Devon side of the Tamar immediately opposite Cotehele. His daughter and heiress married Richard Willoughby, later Lord Willoughby de Broke, who attacked Sir Richard Edgcumbe, but later became his ally.

The large granite object, with a circular bowl cut into a rough cube, and 'lugs' projecting from its sides, apparently to enable it to be lifted, or possibly poured, is a puzzle. It is traditionally thought to be the ancient font of the house, but it is not that shown in Condy's drawing of the Chapel, lying against the foot of the lectern. Possibly the lugs were intended to be carved and the whole set upon a base. It seems more likely that it had some secular purpose.

Crossing the Kitchen Court, re-enter the house past a scullery with Victorian fittings, to reach the Kitchen.

THE KITCHEN

Well placed for the Hall, the Kitchen was less well-sited for the Old Dining Room, when the family ate there. The reconstruction of the east wing in 1862 brought the New Dining Room adjacent to the Kitchen, which continued to be used until the 6th Earl moved into the Stable House at Mount Edgcumbe in 1946, after which it became a store. The nineteenth-century ranges, inserted in the Tudor hearth, were much broken and in 1970 these were removed, the door from the lobby reopened and the room rearranged to accord with its appearance in the middle of the last century, as recorded by Nicholas Condy.

The principal features of the room are its great height (to allow smoke and smells to dissipate through louvred vents – now vanished), the cavernous hearth, 10 feet wide, and the immense oven in the north wall. The Kitchen was used only for cooking and baking. The storage of food, its preparation for the cook and the scouring of pots and pans were carried out in the maze of larders, sculleries and still rooms which lead off the Kitchen Court.

The hearth is furnished with pot hooks for hanging cooking vessels over the fire, with brandises (the West Country name for a trivet) for standing pots over the embers, and with stout iron dogs slanted against the back wall, into which spits for roasting could be fitted. Above the hearth a primitive rack (the same as in Condy's drawing) holds sides of meat and bacon, salted down in the autumn for winter use.

The mysterious square hole in the wall to the left of the hearth may have been to store salt or it may once have penetrated through to the Hall, so that the cook and the steward supervising the serving of meals in the Hall could communicate.

The oven, over 7 feet across and 3 feet high, and a rough oval shape, has a smaller oven beside it. It was heated by lighting a fire of dry sticks, or in poorer households of furze, which flared up quickly, giving intense heat which the walls of the oven absorbed. The ashes were raked out as the fire subsided, the food to be baked inserted and the door closed and sealed with clay. An oven of this size was essential for the large household of a Tudor squire and his retainers.

There is a formidable board of 'Rules to be Strictly Observed', including, 'That the Men at breakfast be allowed one pint of Beer or Cyder

The Kitchen

each, at Dinner and Supper Men and Maids a pint each and Strangers a quart, no other drinking whatever in the Hall or any other part of the House or out Houses under one Shilling forfeit to each offenders.' The board came to Cotehele from Honeycombe, the home of Lady Ernestine for many years; its earlier history is unknown.

The door to the left of the hearth leads into the Lobby.

THE LOBBY

An early photograph shows that this was once an open passageway from the terrace into the house. The window and wall were added, when this entry was closed up. The curving stair to the right of the window, now blocked off, led to rooms on the upper floors used by the servants.

FURNITURE

English dial clock, made by Thos. Hill, London, *c*.1775.

Armchair, mahogany, covered in hide and close-nailed, eighteenth century.

Travelling chest, oak, with domed top, bound with patterned wrought iron, late seventeenth century.

PICTURES

After Sir Joshua Reynolds, PRA (1723–92)
George Edgcumbe, 1st Earl of Mount Edgcumbe (1720/1–95)
Oil on paper stuck down on board
A reduced, and possibly studio, copy of the 1761 portrait at Mount Edgcumbe. The Edgcumbes – George (when the original was begun still plain Commander Edgcumbe), his elder brother, Richard (1716–61), and above all their father, Richard, 1st Lord Edgcumbe (1680–1758) – were among the Plympton-born Reynolds's earliest and most supportive patrons, and the 1st Earl was

painted by him on a number of occasions. At the time when the original of this portrait was painted, he was in command of the *Hero*, and had just taken part in the victorious Battle of Quiberon Bay. Acquired at auction in April 1987.

W. HARDING SMITH (1848–1922)
The Red Room, Cotehele; view from the South
Watercolour
Given by Mrs Hynes in 1984.

JOHN BUCKLER (1770–1851)
View of the Hall, Cotehele
Watercolour
Signed: *J. Buckler 1821*
Worked up from a pencil drawing (dated 22 July 1821) in the British Museum. Acquired in 1976.

JOHN BUCKLER (1770–1851)
View of the South Front, Cotehele
Watercolour
Signed: *J. Buckler 1821*
From the collections of W. G. Dyer and Cyril Staal; given by the NACF in 1983.

NICHOLAS CONDY (?1793–1857)
The Hall at Cotehele with a gamekeeper
Watercolour
Signed and dated 1829
The Cornish-born Condy was a professional soldier, but set up as a painter in Plymouth in 1818, devoting himself chiefly to small watercolours. He is particularly associated with Cotehele, since his best-known painting was *The Old Hall at Cotehele on a Rent-day*, painted for the Earl of Mount Edgcumbe; and he published at his own expense a set of seventeen lithographs entitled *Cothele on the Banks of the Tamar, the ancient seat of the Right Hon. the Earl of Mount Edgcumbe* (with a text supplied by the Rev. F. V. J. Arundell [Jago]).

WILLIAM PAYNE (fl. *c*.1776–1830)
The South Front in the 18th century
Graphite
Purchased in 1986.

Coat of arms of Sir Thomas Coteel of Brabant
Watercolour on vellum
See the portrait of Coteel on the Main Staircase for his biography.

NATHANIEL BEARDMORE
View of Cotehele from the South-East, 1862
Watercolour

NICHOLAS CONDY (?1793–1857)
The Kitchen, *c*.1840
Lithograph

From the Lobby return to the Hall and leave by the main door. Enter the Chapel from the Retainers' Court.

THE CHAPEL

This was built towards the end of the fifteenth century to replace one dedicated to SS. Cyricus and Julitta (a common dedication in Cornwall), which had been erected by Peter Edgcumbe and licensed by the Bishop of Exeter on 12 May 1411. The roof is barrel vaulted with wooden ribs bearing the Tudor rose at the intersections. A notable feature is the contemporary oak screen with carved cusped heads to the openings. The delicate tracery above the panels is thought to be mid-eighteenth-century embellishment, the cresting a Victorian addition. Many of the original Chapel fittings survive, although they underwent restoration in the last century.

As well as the low broad west window for the

The Chapel, c.1840; watercolour by Nicholas Condy (Plymouth City Museum and Art Gallery)

benefit of retainers outside, there are three other views, or 'squints', into the Chapel – a narrow slit from the small room which adjoins to the south, and two from rooms on the first floor, one opening from the Solar (now called the South Room) and the other from the Priest's Room (not open to the public).

STAINED GLASS

The east window was restored in about 1880 by Fouracre & Watson of Plymouth, for little save the coat of arms and the figure of St John had escaped damage. The heraldic panels show the coats of arms of the families of Tremayne, Holland and Durnford, with whom the Edgcumbes married. In the south window the figures of St Catherine on the right and St Anne and the Virgin Mary on the left are thought to be by Anglo-Flemish glaziers working in Southwark or London, c.1520–30.

FLOOR

The floor retains some of its medieval tiles. The green and white glazed tiles in the chancel are early nineteenth-century, attempting to imitate the original colours of the medieval tiles in the nave.

TAPESTRY

ABOVE WEST WINDOW

The Adoration of the Magi
Flemish, early seventeenth century

FURNITURE AND FURNISHINGS

The wooden lectern is a made-up piece, probably dating from the late eighteenth century, ornamented with fragments of sixteenth- and seventeenth-century wood carvings. Some of the linenfold pew ends may have come from the Chapel in the Wood (see p.24).

On either side of the altar stand a pair of seventeenth-century Italian walnut torchères elaborately carved with figures of Our Lord and Saints. The silver candlesticks which stand upon them, each engraved with an image of the Archangel Raphael are probably Flemish, c.1700.

MEMORIALS

Caroline, Countess of Mount Edgcumbe (1808–81)

Lieutenant Piers Edgcumbe (1914–40)
Killed in action at Dunkirk. It originally hung in the Chapel at Mount Edgcumbe and when this was

The Crucifixion, Flemish school, early sixteenth century (Chapel)

dismantled, his sister Lady Hilaria Gibbs asked that it be installed at Cotehele.

Caroline Cecilia, Countess of Mount Edgcumbe (1839–1909)
She married the 4th Earl in the Chapel in 1906.

Kenelm, 6th Earl (1873–1965) and his wife, Lilian (d. 1964)
It was thanks to the 6th Earl that Cotehele came to the National Trust.

Mrs Sheila Breen
Wife of Stanley Breen of Cotehele Farm, who was organist in the Chapel. She made the replacement tatting for the Queen Anne's tatting chair in the Punch Room.

PICTURES

ON THE ALTAR

FLEMISH, late sixteenth century
Triptych, with the Adoration of the Magi and two donors
Panel
Dated (on the wings) 1589
The wings contain portraits of the donor and his wife, with their respective ages, 34 and 28, and what would seem to be his merchant's mark above both. The central panel, which bears the initials *L.B.* (possibly an attempt to pass this off as the work of the Bruges painter-designer, Lancelot Blondeel), may not be the original, as it is painted in a quite different technique, and the three elements could have been framed together some time later to make a suitable devotional object.

SOUTH CHANCEL WALL

FLEMISH, early sixteenth century
Crucifixion
Panel
Recent restoration has revealed the quality of this attractive work – especially in the landscape. It was probably painted in Antwerp, from the early sixteenth century the commercial centre, not just of the Netherlands, but of the Spanish Empire, and a magnet for most Flemish artists.

WEST NAVE WALL

ENGLISH, eighteenth century
The tomb of Sir Richard Edgcumbe at Morlaix
Panel
Sir Richard Edgcumbe died fighting for Anne of Brittany in 1489, and it is there that he was buried. The panel appears to have been based on the watercolour that now hangs on the Main Staircase. John Cornforth has recently suggested that the 1st Earl of Mount Edgcumbe may have had it painted for the Chapel in the Wood built by Sir Richard and restored by the 1st Earl in 1769.

CLOCK

In the south-west corner is the clock installed by Sir Richard Edgcumbe when he completed the chapel between 1485 and 1489. This rare survival is the earliest domestic clock in England still unaltered and in its original position. It is a pre-pendulum clock made entirely of hand-wrought iron and mounted on a stout vertical oak beam, set in a shaft built in the thickness of the wall. This shaft connects with the bellcote above, which contained

The fifteenth-century clock

two bells, one to toll for services and the other to strike the hours. The tolling bell had disappeared long since and was replaced by the National Trust with a bell from Doyden in the Parish of St Minver in 1966. The striking bell is original to the house.

The clock, which has no face, is still in working order and regularly in use during the season. The machinery is controlled by a verge escapement and foliot balance (the mechanism which preceded the more accurate pendulum escapement), and was originally driven by two iron weights, each of about 90 lb. These have been replaced by a single granite weight. The timing can be controlled by two small moveable weights attached to the arms of the bow-shaped foliot balance which moves horizontally, as opposed to the vertical axis of the rest of the mechanism.

CHAPTER NINE
THE GARDEN

In the late eighteenth century the 1st Earl of Mount Edgcumbe laid out an important park and garden in the picturesque manner at Mount Edgcumbe, which were much admired by Uvedale Price and celebrated in verse by David Garrick among others. The garden at Cotehele seems always to have been more modest. In its present form it dates from around 1862 when the formal terraces on the east front of the house were laid out. The tithe maps of 1839 show that the Upper Garden and Nellson's Piece were in use as orchards, and the present Valley Garden was still wooded. In 1820 Gilbert reported that 'the wooded grounds which surround the house are of the grandest description, particularly at that part which is situated between the mansion and the river'. One of the trees was a three-trunked

Spanish Chestnut (*Castanea sativa*), which had a diameter of 11 feet 5 inches before it fell in 1875, and must have been one of the biggest ever to grow in Britain. The gales of 1891, however, so badly damaged the woodlands that the house could be seen from Calstock for the first time in living memory, and it was estimated that 100,000 cubic feet of timber had fallen.

The garden is on many different levels. On the old grey house and the surrounding walls grow some unusual shrubs and climbers, but much of the planting is late Victorian. The Bowling Green lies above the drive approaching the house.

To the left the cobbled way leads through the Retainers' Court with camellias on its walls. On the west wall of the Chapel is a bushy Myrtle (*Myrtus*

The terraced rose garden below the east front

communis). The archway leads to the meadow at the north-west corner of the house. Nineteenth-century engravings show cows being milked here. In spring the grass is a mass of daffodils.

The doorway in the wall to the left leads to the Upper Garden with a square pond fed from a spring by a rill and planted with water lilies. On the lawn below the pond is a Golden Ash (*Fraxinus excelsior* 'Aurea' syn. 'Jaspidea') and big Tulip Tree (*Liriodendron tulipifera*). Within the yew hedges is a cutting garden to provide flowers for the house.

On the lawn above the pond are two young specimens of the Tree of Heaven (*Ailanthus altissima*), planted to replace a casualty of a gale in 1958. The top path runs beside a border of paeonies and fuchsias, the wall behind smothered with ivy,

winter-flowering jasmine and forsythias in the old-fashioned way. This medieval wall continues round the garden and the orchard to the south.

Another doorway, closed by a pierced fretwork door to allow a peep through, leads back into the meadow. To the left is an archway which leads, via a stile, into Tower Field, at the top of which is the Prospect Tower (see below). To the right is a young Cork Oak (*Quercus suber*), planted in 1955 to replace an aged specimen on the other side of the wall, which had collapsed and later had to be removed. The old Judas Tree (*Cercis siliquastrum*), once below the oak, fell in the gales of January 1990; its replacement stands beyond it.

The path leads past a row of White Thorn trees (*Crataegus oxyacantha*), above a Copper Beech

The dovecote

(*Fagus sylvatica* 'Purpurea'), an ancient Mulberry (*Morus nigra*) and another Tulip Tree. To the left of the Tower stands a group of Whitebeams (*Sorbus aria* 'Lutescens'). On the other side is the Dell, now planted with maples, with steps down to the back drive which led to the servants' entrance.

Through the white gate on the left and across the lane is Nellson's Piece, until recently a market garden, but now grassed over to make a place to sit or to picnic. A few yards up the lane a field gate leads into an enclosure where, dug into the bank, is the Ice House in which ice from several ponds was stored for use in the summer.

The garden route, however, continues on the other side of the back drive past a Silver Weeping Lime (*Tilia petiolaris*) to the pointed arch in the north wall of the Terrace Garden. On this wall is a beautiful white wistaria (*Wistaria sinensis alba*).

The three terraces were made in 1862, when the east front of the house was altered. To the left, steps lead to a tunnel under the lane which emerges at the head of the Valley Garden. The path curves down past a large old camellia (*Japonica* 'Elegans') to a thatched Victorian summerhouse overlooking the former medieval stew pond, where fish were kept and fed until needed. It is filled by a spring led into the 'well' below the summerhouse.

Beyond the pond the path leads down the right-hand side of the valley, beside the medieval dovecote and through clumps of *Gunnera manicata*, with immense spiky flower heads in late summer.

The bottom of the valley was planted with spruces, larches and hemlocks as a barrier to shelter the garden from the cold east winds in the spring. The shelter belt was largely destroyed by the 1990 gales and is being replanted. A gate at the foot of the path on the far (south) side leads to the Chapel in the Wood, a single-cell chapel built by Sir Richard Edgcumbe at the end of his life to mark the spot where he hid from Sir Henry Trenowth. The Chapel is on the riverside walk from Calstock, a mile and a half upstream, to Cotehele Quay, half a mile downstream. If the latter route is chosen, there is a drive from the Quay.

The alternative is to return up through the Valley Garden, with views across the tops of the shrubs beside the stream and past the dovecote.

THE DOVECOTE

The dovecote is probably fifteenth-century, made of slatestone rubble with a corbelled roof. Inside is a 'potence', or revolving ladder, for easier access to the higher pigeon holes. Its dome-shaped roof collapsed in about 1860 and was restored by the National Trust a century later. A small family of white doves now inhabits it. The path above the dovecote turns left and emerges through a wicket gate to return to the car-park and the Barn, now the Trust's restaurant and shop.

THE PROSPECT TOWER

In a field immediately north of the house is a three-sided Tower, about 60 feet high and built of the local slatey stone with rough granite pinnacles and pointed dummy windows. It is of three storeys, defined by rough string courses. A stair was inserted by the Trust in 1980 and the Tower may now be ascended by visitors. The walls are dished on each of its three sides, the slight concavity effecting an optical illusion. From a very short distance the Tower appears to be much more solid and church-like than it really is. The Tower commands a wide view, eastwards over the Tamar to Dartmoor, westwards over Cornwall and southwards over Plymouth and Rame Head, with the tower of Maker Church a landmark in the distance.

The origin of the Tower is still uncertain. The local story is that it was built so that the Edgcumbe family could signal to and from Maker Church, which lies at the top of the park at Mount Edgcumbe (only 11 miles away as the crow flies, but a difficult and circuitous journey by road). The Edgcumbes may have used it to warn the servants at either house to prepare for their arrival. It is, more probably, a late eighteenth-century folly, perhaps built to commemorate the visit of George III and Queen Charlotte in August 1789, and Lord Edgcumbe's elevation to an earldom. As Fanny Burney noted in her diary, 'the Edgcumbes were full of the honours done them and told me of the obelisks and arches they meant to construct in commemoration'. Certainly no trace of the projected obelisks and arches remains.

CHAPTER TEN
THE ESTATE

All historians look to Richard Carew's *Survey of Cornwall* (1602) when seeking a neat and accurate description of the county in the late Elizabethan age. His description of Cotehele is typically succinct:

A mile above Halton standeth Cuttayle, from the French Courtaile, in English short-cut; for the salt water course is here straightened by the encroaching banks. The buildings are ancient, large, strong, and fair, and appurtenanced with the necessities of wood, water, fishing, parks and mills, with the devotion of (in times past) a rich furnished Chapel, and with the charity of Alms Houses, for certain poor people, whom the owners used to relieve.

The earliest known map of the estate, dating probably from 1550–60, when the Edgcumbes moved their principal residence to Mount Edgcumbe, helps to give a visual impression of what Richard Carew was describing, although it is simplified to the point of being diagrammatic in places, and it cannot be relied upon for any sense of scale or distance. The map records the vestiges of an old medieval strip-field system in the form of the elongated 'closys' alongside Honycombe House, although by the 1550s it had been enclosed by a hedge or fence. Much of the map is concerned with

The Morden bridge on the Cotehele estate, c.1840, watercolour by Condy (Plymouth City Museum and Art Gallery)

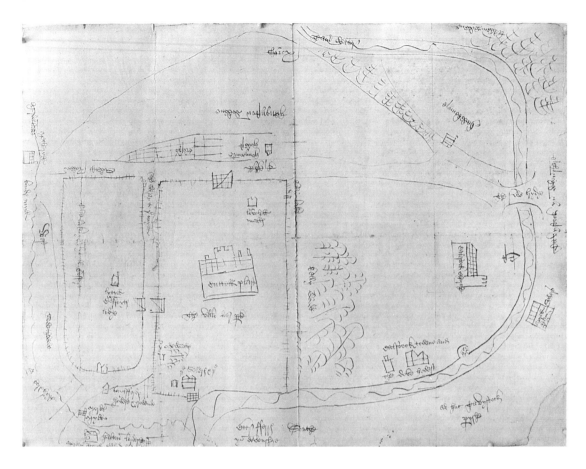

A schematic map of the Cotehele estate, c.1550–60, showing the house at the centre left

the local roads and the network of streams draining into the Tamar (described in the vernacular as 'lakes' on the map and, like the main river course, delineated by sinuous lines). Woods are indicated in similar places to where they are found today, principally between Morden Mill and the house, to the east of the house (Kelly Wode) in the area known as Danescombe, and further to the north at Hawkemore. Much of southern England was seriously deforested in the late sixteenth century to satisfy a great surge in house- and ship-building, but because the region enjoys a plentiful supply of building stone, the woods at Cotehele have survived in a continuous cycle of forestry down to the present day.

A striking feature of the map is the prominence given to gates. Four of them appear on the boundaries of the block of land surrounding the house and that to the west centred on Lyttyl Comforth lodge. These gates, together with the short lines that are drawn across the boundaries, must represent fencing or impalement of the deer park which appears on the map below the house. A deer park is only to be expected on an estate of this importance, but it is perhaps more unusual that it should apparently come right up to the walls of the house on all sides, and that there should be no indication of orchards or formal gardens close to the house. It may simply be, however, that it was not part of the cartographer's brief to include such elements.

A map of 1731 by the surveyor William Doidge and another of 1784 show that by then the present shape of the estate – the roads, drives, park and field systems – had largely been achieved. Of the nine principal farmsteads on the estate today, seven are shown on the 1839 tithe map.

Even before the Industrial Revolution transformed Cornwall with the invention by Richard Trevithick of the high-pressure steam engine, deep mining for lead, tin, copper and their by-products permeated all of Cornwall, and the remains of many mines abound in the wooded Danescombe Valley. Burnt lime was widely used to 'sweeten' the acid West Country soil (previously achieved with sea sand). Barges brought the limestone and culm (coal slack), with which it was burnt, upriver to the lime kilns at Cotehele Quay (see Chapter Eleven). The Quay was also most important for the distribution of fruit which was grown with great success in these moist valleys. In 1796 the agronomist William Mar-

shall found the area to be '... where cherries, pears, walnuts are raised in great abundance for local markets' and estimated that '... all of a thousand pounds worth of fruit, including strawberries ...' was sent out annually from the area.

The specialist nature of the Tamar Valley fruit trade insulated its farmers from the worst effects of the periodic agricultural depressions of the nineteenth century. Labourers too were better placed than many of their contemporaries, because they were used to switching between agriculture, fishing and mining as each industry cycled through good times and bad.

The arrival of the railways in the mid-nineteenth century opened up new markets for early fruit and vegetables. New land was taken in from woodland,

Workers on the Edgcumbe estates, c.1840, by Nicholas Condy (Plymouth City Museum and Art Gallery, Mount Edgcumbe House Collection)

most particularly Comfort Wood which was stripped of mature timber in the First World War.

When the 3rd Earl's widow decided to live permanently at Cotehele in 1862, the farm was wholly reorganised, with a new farmhouse to the south of Sir Richard Edgcumbe's great barn, and a high wall built to shut out the view of the farmyard, with a most comfortable house for the dairy bull behind the north end of the barn. The ground floor of the barn was made into an up-to-date cowshed, with cast-iron partitions between the stalls, and a non-slip, blue-brick floor, with a huge loft over it, and a cider house at the north end. In addition a range of calf houses was built to the east (now the visitors' lavatories), and a traphouse for the steward added to the south end of the barn (now where visitors are received).

At the south end of the orchard a dairy was erected to provide a cottage for the herdsman, quarters for the dairy maids and a modern dairy and dairy scullery where the milk was cooled and butter and cream made daily. This arrangement was in use until the 1960s when the pressure of visitors led to the farm being relocated at Trehill and the barn being converted into the Trust's restaurant and shop, and the dairy into a holiday cottage.

A range of coach-houses was built to the south west of the house, with stables adjoining, and improvements made to the garden, including the lily pond in the upper garden and the tunnel leading from the Terrace Garden in front of the east wing under the cart road to the valley below. Finally, a new supply of water was brought 2 miles from Buddles Adit, which drained a tin mine near St Anne's Chapel, west of Gunnislake. It flowed in an open conduit to the reservoir on the hill to the north of the house and was brought thence by cast-iron pipes to supply the house, the farm and the cottages, and to underground cisterns to provide a reserve of water in case of fire.

The local market garden economy has declined with the strengthening of European agriculture since the Second World War. To compete with the southern European fruit and vegetable growers, farmers must now grow under glass or in plastic tunnels. The steeper land cannot be worked by tractor and is converted to woodland when given up.

Economies of scale have required the amalgamation of smaller holdings, with surplus farmhouses being let for residential use. However, the Trust and its tenants have also invested in new farm buildings, sensitively designed to complement the landscape and be in a position to meet the challenge of agriculture in the 1990s and beyond.

The essential character of the estate's landscape remains intact: a diverse patchwork of grass, arable and market garden fields, about 1,300 acres in all, dotted with cottages and farmsteads, woodlands fringing the steep incised tributary valleys and the Tamar itself.

CHAPTER ELEVEN
THE RIVER, QUAY AND *SHAMROCK*

On the Tamar and its tributaries river transport must have existed from the earliest times. The Benedictine abbey at Tavistock received supplies of cider and dried fish – mackerel, hake and herring – in the thirteenth century, and sea sand, as dressing for the land, was delivered by barge via Morwellham at 6s 8d for a 14-ton load. In the following centuries this river traffic was based on the agriculture and trade of a remote, sparsely populated and largely self-sufficient rural area. Any surplus corn or wool was exported, and products not available locally were imported: coal and iron, for the village blacksmith, a few luxuries for the Mount Edgcumbes, when they were in residence at Cotehele, and sand – later to be superseded by limestone – for sweetening the soil.

At the end of the eighteenth century the use of the river and indeed the whole character of the valley was to change radically as a result of the mining operations when copper production became significant. Mineral production had begun far earlier, as in much of Devon and Cornwall, based chiefly on alluvial deposits of tin. Lead and silver mines in Bere Alston, no more than a mile or two from Cotehele, were being worked by the Crown in the twelfth century, and continued intermittently until the 1860s. Tin deposits were worked as well as manganese, wolfram, arsenic and iron in a broad band which stretched roughly from Callington to Tavistock.

The major part of the valley's mineral production was copper, extracted during the century from

'On the Tamar', by Philip Mitchell, 1845 (private collection). It shows a paddle steamer unloading visitors at Cotehele

about 1770. West Country copper ore was mostly shipped away to smelting works in South Wales and so this became the principal trade, with a procession of schooners plying from crowded quays along the banks of the Tamar. It is difficult to comprehend today, on the peaceful upper reaches around Cotehele, that the largest of dozens of copper mines, Devon Great Consols, exported about 750,000 tons of ore during a period of 55 years, mostly through Morwellham. In the reverse direction, coal, timber, gunpowder and other mine supplies and machinery came upstream. At the other end of the scale, just 300yd from Cotehele Quay, in the woods on the Devon bank, was Ward Mine which produced 130 tons of lead ore and 3900z of silver when it was last worked in the 1870s. The extensive granite and blue elvan quarries and brickworks contributed further traffic to the river.

The presence of the Mount Edgcumbes brought some notable visitors up the Tamar to Cotehele Quay. King George III and Queen Charlotte landed here in 1789, while the Earl was on the Quay in 1846 to greet Queen Victoria on her arrival. In 1865, following a later excursion on the river, the Queen described how:

as we proceeded the scenery became quite beautiful – richly wooded hills, the trees growing down into the water, and the river winding so much as to have the effect of a lake.

The gradual decline of Cotehele as a working quay followed the closure of mines and quarries from the 1870s and the increasing use of mechanised land transport. The population of the valley shrank as the more adventurous miners went off to other parts of the world to apply their skills in the search for new and more productive lodes. Mining villages like Gunnislake went into a decline from which recovery was painfully slow. The railways, which came to Calstock in 1907, took many cargoes from the river, but opened up new outlets for the market garden products of the valley, particularly the local specialities, cherries and strawberries. Fruit from the steep hillsides around Cotehele and Bohetherick no longer went downstream to Plymouth on the market boats, but was taken across the ferry from Cotehele to the Devon bank where a London & South Western Railway wagon would be waiting for the haul up to Bere Alston station, and so to Waterloo and the London markets.

COTEHELE QUAY

There can be little doubt that from the earliest times there has been some form of landing place below Cotehele House. The estate map of the 1550s (see p. 80) shows a building on the site of the quay with the tantalising, incomplete caption: 'Ye Sellers & Ye . . .'. This may refer to cellars associated with fish processing, perhaps for salting the very plentiful river salmon. Alternatively it could apply to a warehouse or store, predecessor of the present building housing the Quay Museum. The earliest depiction of the quay area is an engraving dated 1790 which shows a ship moored on the mud, but no quays. These must have been erected within the next 30 years, for an advertisement in the *Western Luminary Newspaper* of 2 June 1818 describes:

Lime kilns and warehouses on Cotehele Quay for sale consisting of a good dwellinghouse, orchard and garden stored with the choicest fruits, together with a very large and commodious quay, three large lime kilns and a Lime Burner's cottage in an excellent state of repair with very extensive yard, granaries, cellars, stabling and outhouses. The whole forming together the most desirable situation on the river.

To the north, upstream from the quays, stood a boathouse belonging to the Mount Edgcumbes; although smaller, this stood approximately on the site of *Shamrock*'s boatshed, which was erected in 1984–5, probably the first new building here for about 150 years.

The first building on the approach to the quay from downstream is a fine double-fronted house of about 1840. This hides a row of cottages which date from the sixteenth century or possibly earlier, since they incorporate a medieval hall-house. The set of limekilns, close to *Shamrock*'s slipway, was constructed with a lime-burner's cottage attached; this was extended sometime before 1840 and became a public house, with its own brew-house – the house with a castellated tower – behind. The central 'blind' windows of the Edgcumbe Arms would seem to be purely cosmetic, for they coincide with the original external wall.

Lime kilns and lump lime on Cotehele Quay, c.1870

The population at the quay, even with thirsty visiting bargemen, would have produced little enough trade for the Edgcumbe Arms, but it continued to operate until 1880. It may have been closed with others in the locality by Lady Ernestine, sister of the 4th Earl and supporter of the Temperance movement, who lived at Cotehele until about 1905. It was a private dwelling for many years until converted into a tea-room in 1980.

The present quays have been raised over the years. The quay between *Shamrock*'s dock and the boathouse is known as Lime Quay, and was presumably used to unload limestone. The centre quay was used mainly for unloading coal and culm. The lower quay with the crane was used by passengers, and for fruit and vegetables being sent to Plymouth. Downstream of the main quay, beyond the Morden stream, is a subsidiary quay, its wall curved to match the lines of the sailing barges.

The National Trust began a programme in the 1950s to renovate the quay, which had been in slow decline for over a century, establishing a small estate office and using some of the warehouses as estate workshops.

THE TAMAR BARGES

Until the early nineteenth century local traffic on the river was carried by sailing barges. The development of the Tamar barge is difficult to trace, for few records exist of such ordinary working boats; few were registered, apart from the larger 'outside' barges which were able to work beyond the protection of Plymouth breakwater. All were solidly built and bluff-bowed with a reputation for being somewhat unwieldy, with a tendency to capsize. The larger 'outside' barges were designed and rigged in the same way as the local coastal trading smacks and ketches. The design of the smaller 'inside' barges seems to have changed little and the hull shape of *Shamrock*, the last surviving Tamar barge, might have been familiar to the monks of Tavistock Abbey. Single-masted ancestors of *Shamrock*, about 30 feet long and undecked, have certainly sailed the

'The Tamar at Cotehele', by Nicholas Condy, c.1840, when Tamar barges were still a frequent sight on the river (Plymouth City Museum and Art Gallery)

Tamar for centuries. By the late nineteenth century the typical 'inside' barge was about 40 feet in length. Its smack rig incorporated a very large mainsail, the boom overhanging the stern by several feet. The larger barges, some ketch rigged, were 50–60 feet in length. *Shamrock* was not the last Tamar barge to be built, but she is the ultimate development of the design.

The market boats were open and undecked, so the early start from Cotehele or Calstock for Devonport market meant many uncomfortable hours for the travellers, huddled together for shelter amongst the produce of their farms – chickens and pigs, vegetables, butter and cheese. The survival of undecked barges into this century is the more surprising as even a decked sailing boat can be difficult to propel on a winding river. When the wind failed,

planks had to be laid across the thwarts so that the barge could be punted or rowed along. It was logical, therefore, to cover the hold permanently, with the added advantages in seaworthiness when working out in the more choppy waters of Plymouth Sound.

THE PASSENGER STEAMERS

Early in the last century the pattern of shipping on the river changed with the coming of steam-powered vessels. New paddle steamers could provide a regular and quicker service, less dependent on tide and weather. Leaving Calstock at 7am, rather than in the middle of the night, perishable fruit could arrive for the morning markets of Plymouth and Devonport, while steamer excursions on the Tamar became one of the most popular pastimes for Victorian and Edwardian Plymothians. The heyday of the paddle steamer fleets lasted from about 1860 until the First World War when often as many as a thousand 'excursionists' would arrive at Calstock on a summer Sunday; others stopped off at Cotehele or travelled on to Morwellham or Weir Head. The strawberry and cream tea trade and the numerous public houses flourished. Rival companies competed for business, fares being reduced to 1/- return from Plymouth to Calstock in the 1860s. Disasters were narrowly avoided, although groundings occurred, as vessels raced to river bends or to tie up first at a landing place.

The excursion business never recovered from the First World War; a few boats returned to run as market boats, but pleasure trips were hard hit by the new motor buses and charabancs. By about 1929 the 115-foot *Empress*, the last paddle steamer, was replaced by motor vessels, whose successors continue to ply the river, usually to Calstock; during the season they frequently stop at Cotehele Quay, to unload visitors for the house.

SHAMROCK

Shamrock was built for Tom Williams, a Torpoint lighterman, by Frederick Hawke of Stonehouse, Plymouth, and first registered on 4 September 1899. Tom's son, Harry, suggested that his father went to Hawke with the idea of a flat-bottomed barge, and drop-keels were added to restore some lateral resistance when sailing. She was therefore completely different from other barges and unique amongst small merchant vessels of the period, but at the same time was the logical development of the Tamar barge, able to carry the maximum cargo with the minimum draft. The shallow draft had advantages on the river, working to shallow creeks on the tide, ahead of deeper drafted barges. It also proved most useful for her regular calls at Torpoint where *Shamrock* could be run on to the beach and remain upright, loading and unloading direct from each side.

During the next 20 years she worked inside Plymouth Breakwater, on the Tamar and its tributaries, carrying limestone from Pomphlet Lake and coal for some of the surviving limekilns on the river. She carried bricks, possibly from works which adjoined the canal at Weir Head, below Gunnislake, and certainly from the Southdown brickworks on Millbrook Lake for builders in Torpoint, who also needed sand which could be dredged from the river-bed at Pentillie. *Shamrock*'s shallow draft again proved an advantage for this work.

'Shamrock' in the 1920s

Her most regular cargoes continued the family connection with the Western Counties & General Manure Co., on whose barge *Garland* young Tom had been crew to his father, for many years her master. *Shamrock* sailed the short crossing from their works at Torpoint to the L&SWR's Ocean Quay, carrying fertilizer. In 1907 Tom's younger brother, Fred Williams, became half-owner and officially her master. On the outbreak of the First World War, *Shamrock* began carrying 18lb shells from Plymouth Sound to Ocean Quay.

With the arrival of the railway and improved road transport after the First World War freight traffic on the Tamar rapidly disappeared, and with it *Shamrock*'s traditional livelihood. Only 20 years old, she was sold into one of the few trades where there was a demand for these old shallow draft wooden barges. Ironically, *Shamrock* was to carry roadstone for the next 42 years of her life. A group of quarry-owners with stone quarries on the Lynher River bought her for £600 in July 1919. She was given an auxiliary engine and strengthened for her new task, which involved extensive coastal work as far down as Falmouth and the Lizard.

In 1962 she was sold again, this time for drilling and dredging for tin ore in St Ives Bay, and finally, between 1966 and 1970, she was used for salvage work on wrecks in Mount's Bay and the adjoining coast, before being abandoned in Hoe Lake, the ships' graveyard for Plymouth.

Shamrock had completed a working life of over 70 years, and lay semi-derelict, but she was now recognised as a unique survival of a West Country river barge. At the same time the National Trust was restoring Cotehele Quay to its nineteenth century appearance, and seeking an appropriate vessel to complete the scene. The National Maritime Museum considered that the restoration of *Shamrock* would provide useful information on the restoration and long-term maintenance of a wooden vessel using entirely traditional materials and methods. *Shamrock*'s simple, though heavy, construction and modest size made her an ideal vessel in many ways for such an experiment, while the sheltered river and adjoining coasts would make it possible for *Shamrock* to be sailed, an interesting exercise for the Museum, and an opportunity for the Trust to breathe more life into the quay at Cotehele. With temporary patches in her leaking hull, *Shamrock* returned to the Tamar, under tow, and arrived at Cotehele Quay on 25 March 1974.

It had been decided that the vessel would be rigged as she appeared in 1926, so a new mizzen mast and new spars were required, as well as running rigging and sails, for *Shamrock* was virtually stripped above deck level. The outer planking was in a poor state, requiring replacement, but the degree of hidden decay in the frames and other timbers could only be guessed. As work began, and old timbers were exposed, it was found that most of the 35 oak frames were in an advanced state of decay with wet rot and bad corrosion from the iron fastenings. A complex operation, which amounted to taking the bottom of *Shamrock* apart, was needed to assess and replace timbers where necessary.

Mr T. Perkins, shipwright in charge, stripping 'Shamrock's' hull prior to restoration

'Shamrock' today

For the accurate and complete restoration to her original full ketch-rig of 1920–38, with bowsprit, old members of her crew had been located, including Richard Hoskings, her master in the late 1920s, who by then was 94 years old. Vital photographic evidence was also collected for the Museum archive. The National Trust and the National Maritime Museum were now convinced that restoration should continue using exclusively traditional materials and quality timber, such as English elm for planking below the waterline.

The full rigging of *Shamrock* required materials and fittings no longer available, and an extensive search was made of abandoned hulls, old boatyards and ships' chandlers from Cornwall to Essex. Shackles and blocks were found in Southampton; well-seasoned oregon pine spars were purchased in London; best manila rope was specially ordered from British Ropes Ltd, and sufficient flax canvas, bolt ropes and cringles acquired for the new suit of traditional hand-stitched sails, which were made up by Penrose Sailmakers of Falmouth, makers of *Shamrock*'s last mainsail in the 1930s.

By mid-1977 nearly all framing of the hull was completed and the outer planking could now be replaced, careful trimming of the inner frame faces

being essential so that planking, acting as a stressed skin, would form an integral part of the structure of the vessel. Work on the deck began with straight-grained 2in larch and Douglas Fir, its edges bevelled to allow for caulking with countersunk holes to take the metal spike fastenings, plugged with tight-fitting fir dowels. Caulking the planks with spunyarn, then oakum well hardened down, then hot pitch, was both a skilled and lengthy task. Early in 1979 work started on masting and rigging the vessel. After four years and ten months on the slip-way, *Shamrock* was floated off the cradle on the evening tide of 26 April 1979.

The new sails arrived from Falmouth in July to be stretched and proofed with a bees-wax-based solution, before being bent on and hoisted for the first time to complete her authentic appearance. A new chapter in the long life of *Shamrock* had been opened.

Finally, *Shamrock* had to prove herself at sea. After some trials in Plymouth Sound, she set sail in 1983 to visit Fowey, a repeat of her maiden voyage in the summer of 1899. Now she is regularly used on the Tamar, with an occasional longer voyage to visit some of her former ports of call along the south coasts of Devon and Cornwall.

CHAPTER TWELVE
THE MILL

The Morden stream runs into the Tamar just below the quay. Half a mile up its picturesque valley is the manor mill of the Cotehele estate, which has been in use since early medieval times. The present building was probably constructed in different phases during the eighteenth century, and the mill house (which is not open to visitors) dates from the nineteenth century. The water supply is taken from the Morden stream; a leat, controlled by two sluices, brings it from a weir pool about 400yd upstream. The mill was in regular use until 1964, latterly for grinding of corn for cattle feed. The mill machinery has recently been put in order and that part of the building nearest the road, once used as a bakery, now houses the traditional West Country cider house. The outbuildings to the east contain a blacksmith's forge and wheelwright's, saddler's and carpenter's shops.

THE WHEELWRIGHT'S SHOP

The twin-arched doorways on the right open into the shed used for wagons and carts under repair. This leads into the shop itself where the most important piece of apparatus is the lathe under the far window. The lathe was driven by the great wheel fixed against the long wall on the right and turned by hand. It was used to shape wheel hubs made of elm, and also called naves or stocks. The wheel spokes, usually made from split oak, were driven into the hub on the spoking horse, which stands immediately to the right of the entrance. Next came very careful checking of the spoke lengths to ensure that the wheel would be perfectly round, and the making and fitting of the felloes (the several parts of the rim), after which the wheel was ready for the fitting of the iron tyre and hoops on the hub. For this highly skilled operation the blacksmith's assistance was essential.

Most wheelwrights, especially those working for an estate, did many other jobs. They often built carts or wagons, and made the wooden parts needed for horse harness called pommel-trees and whipple-trees, and all the smaller things of a like kind used on farms.

Through the door on the left is the Blacksmith's Forge.

THE BLACKSMITH'S FORGE

Practically all the estate metalwork was done here. The blacksmith not only shod horses and tyred wheels, but also made all small metal objects such as hinges and latches – even iron nails. The forge is blown by a pair of round bellows worked with the left hand. The anvil is set conveniently to the smith's right so that as little heat as possible is lost in transferring the iron from fire to anvil. Under the window is a bench with vice, and elsewhere a drilling machine and a bender. The cow's horn on the end of the bellow lever seems to have been traditional, as it gives a good grip, stays clean and smooth, and is very hard-wearing. Another pair of pear-shaped bellows, stored up in the roof, is of an older type, and was superseded by the round bellows. When horses are to be shod, they are led in by the bottom door and tied up to the rings on the wall opposite the forge; afterwards they can be taken out by the top door. In fine weather shoeing can be done outside.

In the paved yard at the back of the forge are a grindstone for sharpening and shaping tools, and a wheel-binding plate. The latter was used to carry red-hot iron tyres out from the forge. The wooden wheel was then laid flat on the plate and water from the nearby water butt poured over to shrink the tyre to fit the wheel tightly.

Nearby is the stone-faced sawpit. Before the days

The sawpit, with the blacksmith's forge beyond

of mechanical saws all timber had to be sawn from the log by hand. The top-sawyer guided the saw from above, the bottom-sawyer stood beneath to pull the saw on its downward stroke, and then to lift up again ready for the next stroke – an arduous and dusty task.

Walk up the slope towards the Mill. Turning to the left, the visitor enters the Saddler's Shop.

THE SADDLER'S SHOP

Until sixty years ago, when the tractor began to displace the horse, the saddler was an essential crafts-man on any country estate. The steep slopes of the Tamar valley called for strong harness for the work-

ing horses, both on the farms and in the woods. As well as new saddles, head collars, girths and bridles there was a steady demand for repairs, and the sad-dler was an expert at cobbling up old harness for the small farmers who could not afford new.

In the corner is a treadle-operated sewing machine, and under the window a bench fitted with vice and punch. Against the far wall another bench has a special wooden knee vice for holding harness while it was being finished, and a stout screw press. Above the bench is the saddler's rule, fitted with calipers, for measuring the horse's body to give a snug fit.

Along the shelf on the right-hand wall are set out stoneware bottles containing harness dressing, leather stain and burnishing ink. Beside the door, leather leggings, often made by the country saddler, are stacked above the primitive chest of drawers which held the crooks and shanks, the hooks and studs, the buckles and keepers with which the saddler fitted his wares.

Leave by the entrance door, turn left and take the next door into the Carpenter's Shop.

THE CARPENTER'S SHOP

The bench on the left is furnished with hand tools much the same as those used by a carpenter today. On the wooden boarding above the end wall are hung thatcher's tools. The wooden half-hoop is used to carry up to the roof the wheat straw for thatching (known as reed in the West Country). The wooden mallets with toothed faces, or drifts, are used to beat the thatch tight and smooth after it has been laid and before it is pegged with hazel spars. The square mallet is known as a leggett. The rectangular wooden frames with curved iron spikes (biddles) provided a moveable step for the thatcher on the steep slope of the roof.

On the small bench underneath is a hand paint grinder, used in the days when each estate mixed its own paints from earth colours, or from natural materials such as the yellow ochre used to tint limewash. It was also used for grinding dried-up remnants of paint for reuse. The heavy cast-iron bandsaw by F. W. Reynolds and Co. is of this century and is hand-turned by means of the flywheel. On the far wall is the timber rack, used to store the timber brought in from the seasoning stack for the joiner. Behind the bench under the window is a fitted box containing the stocks and dies used for turning threads on iron bolts. On the sloping board to the right are mounted saws of several shapes, including a frame saw used for cutting curves in timber. Beside the door the mortice machine performed the cutting of mortices into which the tenon is fitted in making joints.

Follow the drive past the Mill House. In the yard the door immediately in front is to the Cider House.

THE CIDER HOUSE

Inside the door on the right is the donkey wheel that provided power for the crusher into which apples were fed from the floor above. Immediately opposite is the great press. Apple pulp descending from the crusher was built up between layers of straw on the wooden tray or vat into a cheese.

The cider press

The waterwheel of Cotehele Mill

When this was complete and trimmed, the press was screwed down, the first part of it to come into contact with the cheese being named the sow, and the transverse beam just above that, the boar.

The door to the right of this leads out to the rear of the mill where a good view is obtained of the mill wheel and the leat overflow, the wooden conduit bringing a flow of water to the wheel which can be controlled from inside the mill. This is an overshot system, i.e. the water propels the wheel by descending on it from above.

Return through the Cider House to the yard where the next exterior door leads into the Mill.

THE MILL

On the ground floor is the machinery of the main drive which transmitted power to the floor above. The lowest wheel, called the pit wheel, works directly off the drive from the waterwheel and engages with the large spur wheel and pinion gear. Most driving wheels are fitted with wooden cogs and these are usually of apple, beech, or chestnut. Holly is also used where there is a danger that severe damage would result if a cog shears, as it shears with a clean break, unlike most other woods.

Return to the yard and ascend to the upper floors by the exterior stone staircase.

The grinding room contains two sets of stones. The rotating upper stone, without a cover, is of a type known as a French Burr (Buhr) stone, suitable for milling flour and imported in large quantities from France. (The granite stones often seen outside West Country mills were normally used for grinding cattle feed.) Only the runner stone revolves. The gap between the stones is adjustable from the floor below. The shutes leading into the hopper over the stones are connected to two large wooden storage bins on the floor above where corn for milling was received. (This floor is not shown.)

The large wheel on the main shaft is the crown wheel, which transmits power to the auxiliary drives known as lay shafts. The right-hand lay shaft drives an electric generator, now sixty years old but in working order, a dust extractor and the sack hoist which is situated at the top of the mill. The other lay shaft drives an auger for mixing cattle food.

BIBLIOGRAPHY

COTEHELE

ARUNDELL, Rev. F.V.J. [Jago], *Cothele, on the banks of the Tamar, the ancient seat of the Rt. Hon. the Earl of Mount Edgcumbe, c.*1840 [with hand-coloured lithographs by Nicholas Condy]

CORNFORTH, John, 'Cotehele House, Cornwall – I and II', *Country Life*, clxxxiv, 1 and 8 February 1990, pp. 52–5, 68–71

HUSSEY, Christopher, 'Cotehele House, Cornwall – I and II', *Country Life*, lvi, 30 August, 6 September 1924, pp. 324–31, 360–8

LEES-MILNE, JAMES, *Caves of Ice*, 1983

MOUNT EDGCUMBE, the 4th Earl of, *Records of the Edgcumbe Family*, 1888

WAINWRIGHT, Clive, 'Only the true black blood', *Furniture History*, xxi, 1985, pp. 250–7

WAINWRIGHT, Clive, *The Romantic Interior*, Yale, 1989

SHAMROCK

BOOKER, Frank, *The Industrial Archaeology of the Tamar Valley*, David & Charles, 1967

KITTERIDGE, ALAN, *Passenger Steamers of the River Tamar*, 1984

MERRY, Ian, *The Shipping and Trade of the River Tamar*, National Maritime Museum, 1980

VINER, Alan, *The restoration of the ketch-rigged Tamar sailing barge Shamrock 1974–79*, National Maritime Museum, 1983

The south front of Cotehele, c.1840, watercolour by Nicholas Condy (Plymouth City Museum and Art Gallery)

INDEX